Finding God in
IT'S A
WONDERFUL
LIFE

Endorsements

"I've treasured Greg Asimakoupoulos for many years as a friend and always come away inspired and enriched by him. Greg is blessed with the ability to find meaning in life's challenges, along with the gift of expressing those lessons in an entertaining and profound way through his writings and his homilies."

> Gregg Hersholt—morning anchor at KOMO Newsradio
> and grandson of Jean Hersholt
> (*Hollywood film legend*)

Frank Capra's crown jewel, *It's A Wonderful Life*, owns a piece of America's heart. Rescreening this touching tale through the lens of poet/pastor Greg Asimakoupoulos fills that heart with gratitude to Philip Van Doren Stern whose short story, "The Greatest Gift," inspired the movie. If you love George Bailey and the people of Bedford Falls, give yourself and others "the gift" of Greg's redeeming reflections.

> George Toles (*advertising executive*)

Finding God in
IT'S A WONDERFUL LIFE

Greg Asimakoupoulos

Published by eChristian, Inc.
Escondido, California

eChristianBooks

Finding God in *IT'S A WONDERFUL LIFE*

First printing in 2012 by eChristian, Inc.
eChristian, Inc.
2235 Enterprise Street, Suite 140
Escondido, CA 92029
http://echristian.com

ISBN: 978-1-61843-305-3

Cover and interior design by Larry Taylor.

Produced with the assistance of Livingstone, the Publishing Services Division of eChristian, Inc. Project staff includes: Molly Anderson, Dan Balow, Lois Jackson, Lisanne Kaufmann, Afton Rorvik, Linda Taylor, Ashley Taylor, and Tom Shumaker.

Printed in the United States of America

19 18 17 16 15 14 13 12 8 7 6 5 4 3 2 1

Contents

Foreword

Few movies have impacted American culture like Frank Capra's classic film *It's a Wonderful Life*. When it was released in 1946, it ironically did not have a wonderful reception. Critics gave it mixed reviews. Although nominated for five Academy Awards (including best picture), the film did not garner a single gold statue.

But six decades later, *It's a Wonderful Life* has claimed a place in the soul of our nation. The feel-good story of a good man who wonders if his life is a mistake, only to be shown how bad the world would be without him, connects with common people.

I first saw *It's a Wonderful Life* in 1975. My cousin had seen the film in a small vintage theatre in Seattle and had been deeply moved by the message. Knowing my proclivity for heartwarming movies, Dan encouraged me to go. I did.

The simple, yet profound, story of George Bailey awakened a sense of life's sacredness. What had been slumbering within me began to stir. It was a time in my life when I was struggling with direction and purpose.

I had graduated from a Christian college and taken a job in public relations but wasn't really sure where I was headed. I had big dreams but lacked specific goals. I had no significant other (and none on the horizon), so loneliness was a constant companion. It was the melancholy temperament with which I had been born. On low days, I wondered if my life really mattered to anybody.

The character portrayed by Jimmy Stewart drew me in. I identified with George Bailey. I empathized with his crisis of worth. And by the time the movie was over, I was celebrating his renewed sense of purpose. For me it truly was a religious experience.

Within a year or so my life's calling clarified and I went on to seminary and became pastor at a small congregation in Washington State. In my Christmas messages I would often make reference to scenes from what I now considered my favorite movie.

When I did marry, I introduced my wife to a film that had become part of my Christmas festivities as a bachelor pastor. Gratefully, Wendy embraced the movie's appeal along with me. When our three daughters reached an age where they could articulate our traditions at Christmastime, they recognized that watching IAWL was as much a part of the season as singing carols, baking cookies, attending church services, and opening gifts.

As our little family moved to California and to Illinois, our miniature Bedford Falls village graced our home each December while IAWL ornaments hung from our Christmas tree.

Upon returning to Seattle after a couple of decades away, I had the opportunity to meet the person who played Zuzu Bailey in the movie. Karolyn Grimes, who was approaching seventy years of age, lived nearby. I was thrilled, to say the least.

So when I was approached about writing a book about *It's a Wonderful Life*, I felt as though I had been awarded my wings. What could be more meaningful than reflecting on something that had become so much a part of my life?

Let me be clear from the outset, *It's a Wonderful Life* is not a "Christian" movie. But it is filled with countless spiritual values. It's a film that focuses on the meaning of life, the value of each individual, the rewards associated with self-sacrifice, the indispensability of community, and the interconnectedness of the human family.

Finding God in It's a Wonderful Life is an invitation to look for "God sightings" on each page. As with the *Where's Waldo?* books my kids used to peruse by the hour looking for a bespeckled little man in a red and white striped shirt and cap, finding God will require some concentration and focus. But I assure you, it will be well worth the effort.

At the end of each chapter are questions intended to spark personal reflection or small group discussion. They are aimed at providing you with tangible ways to act on the values pictured in the movie and described in this book.

FINDING GOD

Finding God in Bedford Falls?
By George, I have. Will you?
Like Waldo He keeps showing up
amid the many clues.
He's there at old man Gower's store.
and in the Granville home.
You'll find Him there at Harry's prom
or as George prays alone.
He's there beside young Zuzu's bed
and at Martini's bar.
To find the Lord within this film,
you need not look that far.
He's there when Mr. Potter tries
to trap George in his web.
And He is there when George gives up
and wishes he was dead.
Although you'll never see His face,
God's fingerprints abound
within this movie millions love.
The plot is holy ground!

—Greg Asimakoupoulos

A View from Heaven's Front Porch

It's a Wonderful Life opens with scenes from a small town on Christmas Eve. As the snow falls, voices are heard. A number of townsfolk from Bedford Falls are praying for George Bailey.

The camera pans the sky and focuses on bright lights pulsating in the galaxy. A conversation is heard between a couple of heavenly beings. We aren't entirely sure who Joseph and Franklin are, but they represent the divine perspective of what's occurring on earth. Franklin appears to be Joseph's supervisor.

> *Hello, Joseph, trouble?*
> *Looks like we'll have to send someone down—a lot of people are asking for help for a man named George Bailey.*
> *George Bailey. Yes tonight's his crucial night. You're right. We'll have to send someone down immediately. Whose turn is it?*

Joseph seems somewhat apologetic as he informs Franklin that the heavenly being going to help George is a watchmaker by the name of Clarence. They muse over this angel-in-training who has not yet earned his wings. Both agree he has the IQ of a rabbit yet possesses the simple faith of a child.

And with that knowledge they call for Clarence who responds.

> *"You sent for me, sir?"*
> *"Yes, Clarence,"* Franklin answers. *"A man down on earth needs our help."*

"Splendid! Is he sick?"

"No, worse. He's discouraged. At exactly ten-forty-five PM tonight, Earth time, that man will be thinking seriously of throwing away God's greatest gift."

Clarence may be naïve, but he knows that God's greatest gift is a person's life. And he is ready to deploy as an ambassador of hope.

Obviously, the theology of the opening scene is suspect. Nowhere in the Bible are we led to believe that human beings become angels when they take their leave from terra firma. And no chapter and verse states that angels have to earn their wings. Or that all angels have wings, for that matter.

But Scripture is quite clear about the fact that our lives as human beings are observed from the heavenly realm. God sees what is going on and is moved by what he sees.

Many scholars believe that the Old Testament story of Job is the oldest book in the Bible. If that is true, it provides us with an ancient peek at God's perspective toward his creation.

The writer of Job conveys the truth of his message in the form of a drama. In the opening scene of the first act, the Lord God is carrying on a conversation with a fallen angel by the name of Satan.

> *One day the angels came to present themselves before the Lord, and Satan also came with them. The Lord said to Satan, "Where have you come from?" Satan answered the Lord, "From roaming throughout the earth, going back and forth on it." Then the Lord said to Satan, "Have you considered my servant Job? There is no one on earth like him; he is blameless and upright, a man who fears God and shuns evil." (Job 1:6-8)*

Like Franklin and Joseph's view of George Bailey, the Lord was completely aware of Job's life. He knew the integrity and moral character of this husband, father, and businessman. He had observed his dealings with family members and friends. And because of his firsthand knowledge, he was in a position to brag to Satan about Job.

In the case of Job, crisis and calamity formed the backdrop of the story of a man who questioned his worth, his ability to trust God, and his friends, all the while dealing with unimaginable heartache. But in the end, justice prevailed, and God came through. Job discovered just how wonderful his life really was in spite of the pain and suffering he was allowed to experience. Part of what made it wonderful was knowing that God was an active observer of his life.

Moses also discovered that God had a ringside seat as his people were being pummeled by the right hooks and upper cuts of Egyptian slavery. He came to be aware heaven was watching.

Remember when he was in the Sinai wilderness tending sheep? A bush caught fire. As he came closer to the crackling branches, Moses couldn't believe his eyes. He saw fire, smoke, and felt the heat, but the bramble bush wasn't burning. Then he heard a voice commanding him to remove his sandals.

In Exodus 3, we read, "The LORD said, 'I have indeed seen the misery of my people in Egypt. I have heard them crying out because of their slave drivers, and I am concerned about their suffering'" (v. 7).

The Lord was aware. He could see as well as hear what was going on in the lives of his people. Nothing escaped his vantage point. And God was moved by what he witnessed. He didn't send an angel-in-training; instead, he empowered a shepherd he'd engaged in conversation at the burning bush.

The psalm writer has experienced in his own life what Moses discovered at the blazing bramble. God is not blind to what blindsides us. Nothing escapes the all-seeing eye.

Psalm 139 extols this firsthand knowledge of the Creator.

> You have searched me, LORD, and you know me. You know when I sit and when I rise; you perceive my thoughts from afar. You discern my going out and my lying down; you are familiar with all my ways. Before a word is on my tongue you, LORD, know it completely. (vv. 1-4)

When Jesus came on the scene in the first century, he wanted those he taught to know that the divine audience of the earth was still watching. Although a five-hundred-year intermission had occurred during which time no prophet had spoken to God's people, Jesus was quick to remind his listeners that what was true for Job and Moses and the psalmist was still true. The Lord is an active observer.

In Matthew 6, Jesus reminds his followers that the Father knows their needs:

> So do not worry, saying, "What shall we eat?" or "What shall we drink?" or "What shall we wear?" For the pagans run after all these things, and your heavenly Father knows that you need them. (vv. 31-32)

In Luke 12, Jesus reiterates the Father's knowledge of his creation. It is so complete, he actually knows the number of hairs we have on our heads. If the Creator can see a wounded sparrow fall to the ground, he has 20/20 vision that can easily see the changes in our lives.

As we approach the last pages of our Bible, we are once again reminded of the fact that our joys and struggles on earth are not for our eyes only. Our laughter, tears, trials, and triumphs are not hidden from those who have finished their race and now rest on their laurels.

The unidentified author of Hebrews provides a very graphic portrait of how the inhabitants of heaven look down on our world. The epistle pictures a stadium in heaven akin to those used in the first century Olympic Games. The grandstands are crowded with the heroes of the faith mentioned in the eleventh chapter. The likes of Abraham, Joseph, Moses, Rahab, and Daniel are seated side by side. They are peering down on those humans still running the race of faith. It reads in chapter 12:

> Therefore, since we are surrounded by such a great cloud of witnesses, let us throw off everything that hinders and the sin that so easily entangles. And let us run with perseverance the race marked out for us. (v. 1)

Yes, the opening scene of Frank Capra's movie introduces us to a timeless truth: No matter what it is that is going on in our lives, God is aware of it and has the resources to help us deal with our needs. If you're interested in finding God in *It's a Wonderful Life*, you don't have to look far or wait long.

SAVING HARRY BAILEY

Following the opening scene of the movie where family and friends fervently pray for George Bailey, Clarence the angel is given a peek into George's childhood. The year is 1919. We see a twelve-year-old George sledding with his chums on a snowy hillside outside Bedford Falls.

The boys take turns using large shovels to slide down the hill toward a frozen river. When it's his little brother's turn, George calls up to Harry, "Here comes the scare baby, my kid brother Harry Bailey."

Harry, determined to prove his big brother wrong, counters, "I'm not scared!"

As Harry slides down the hill, however, his shovel gathers speed. The boy travels beyond the markers where the others have stopped and ends up at a bend in the river where the ice is thin. Harry and the shovel fall through into the frigid water.

George, sensing the life-threatening circumstances, races to Harry, jumps in the icy water, and grabs him to keep him from going under. George calls for the others to form a human chain. As the boys lay on their stomachs linked together, both Harry and George are pulled to safety. As a result of diving in the cold water to save his brother's life, George gets a serious infection in his left ear that causes him to lose his hearing.

Years later, when George and Harry's father dies of a stroke, George acquiesces to the wishes of the Bailey Building and Loan board of directors and takes over running the company instead of going to college. Then he gives the money he saved to pay for his college education to his brother Harry, while he stays behind. Denying his own desires, he makes it possible for his brother to pursue his plans.

This demonstration of putting others before ourselves calls to mind the ultimate example of self-sacrifice. The one who invited his followers to deny themselves and take up a cross, demonstrated this firsthand.

Jesus, the sinless Son of God, did not deserve the unjust death inflicted on him. The cross he embraced and on which he died had our names on it. Genetically flawed and predisposed to sin, we were the ones deserving death.

But, like the image of a twelve-year-old George Bailey, Jesus gave his life to save us from the frigid water of sin in which we were helplessly drowning. He willingly surrendered his glory to reach down and rescue us.

Jesus put aside his rights and privileges in order to qualify us for a life to which we had no legitimate claim. In Philippians 2, the apostle Paul describes the self-effacing love Jesus demonstrated in coming to our needy world.

> *Do nothing out of selfish ambition or vain conceit. Rather, in humility value others above yourselves, not looking to your own interests but each of you to the interests of the others. In your relationships with one another, have the same mindset as Christ Jesus: Who, being in very nature God, did not consider equality with God something to be used to his own advantage; rather, he made himself nothing by taking the very nature of a servant, being made in human likeness. And being found in appearance as a man, he humbled himself by becoming obedient to death—even death on a cross!* (vv. 3-8)

That picture of preferring others above ourselves is what we see in the movie when George stays in Bedford Falls in order to allow his brother to go to college ahead of him.

But Jesus did not only demonstrate self-sacrifice, he demanded that those of us who consider ourselves his disciples actually follow his lead. As he neared the end of his earthly ministry, Jesus told his followers, "My command is this: Love each other as I have loved you. Greater love has no one than this: to lay down one's life for one's friends" (John 15:12-13).

In June of 1968, Dr. Jim Reddick actually did just that. Along with his twelve-year-old daughter and eleven-year-old son, the Seattle dentist set out to climb 14,000 foot Mt. Rainier. Dr. Reddick was making good on a promise he had made to Sharon and David a year before. As they reached the 9,000 foot level on Friday, the threesome encountered an unexpected storm of blinding snow and sixty mile-an-hour winds.

When the temperature plummeted, Dr. Reddick told his children they would have to dig in fast and make a shelter. Turning their backs to the blizzard they started to scoop out a cave with their mess kit plates. The trio was making good progress, but before they could carve a cave large enough for all three of them to fit in, the wind grew worse and their little cave started to fill up with drifting snow.

Because the makeshift cave had room for only one sleeping bag, the loving father ordered the kids to crawl into it. With no space inside, Dr. Reddick curled up in his bag at the entrance to the cave, his body serving as a protective shelter from the wind, snow, and cold.

The kids' dad distracted them from the fearful ordeal by telling them stories, relating Bible verses and leading them in songs and prayer. From time to time he would reach with his exposed hand and give the children's sleeping bag a squeeze to reassure them. But when several hours passed without another squeeze from that big hand, Sharon and David feared the worst. Come Sunday when a search party discovered the cave, the kids' fears were realized. Their dad had given his life to save theirs.

The dramatic story of the Reddick family is a sad (but inspiring) example of self-sacrifice. All the same, laying down our lives for our friends and family doesn't necessarily mean dying that they might live.

What Jesus had in mind is more like what the apostle Paul describes in that passage from Philippians already referenced.

> *Do nothing out of selfish ambition or vain conceit. Rather, in humility value others above yourselves, not looking to your own interests but each of you to the interests of the others. (2:3-4)*

This laying down of one's life is more of a death to ego. It means developing a lifestyle that is characterized by the pattern of putting others first. That's how Jesus loved us and that is how he says our love for others can be measured. Once again, Paul had a way of putting it succinctly. In his letter to the first century believers in Rome he writes, "Be devoted to one another in love. Honor one another above yourselves" (Romans 12:10).

If only that way of life was as easy to practice as it is to preach. But to the degree that we get a handle on it, we can make a wonderful life for others as well as ourselves.

QUESTIONS FOR REFLECTION:

1. The motif of self-sacrifice is a popular one in motion pictures. What examples can you think of?

2. When did you deny yourself something to which you were entitled (and perhaps to which you were looking forward)? What was the payoff?

3. Why do you think self-denial is the cornerstone of love for Jesus?

4. How can you serve others today?

Chapter 2

ASK DAD. HE KNOWS!

Young George Bailey is faced with a dilemma. His employer, Mr. Gower, is obviously drunk. His unshaven face and disheveled clothing indicate something is going on.

While working behind the soda fountain, George happens on a telegram that explains his boss's odd behavior. The wire from Hammerton College is addressed to Mr. Gower.

"We regret to inform you that your son, Robert, died very suddenly this morning of influenza stop. Everything possible was done for his comfort stop. We await instructions from you."

When George discovers Mr. Gower in the back room, the old man is attempting to put capsules in a medicine bottle but spills some on the floor. As George attempts to help, he discovers that the powder his employer has put in the capsules is from a bottle labeled "poison."

When Mr. Gower demands that George deliver the prescription to Mrs. Blaine, George isn't sure what to do. He knows he should obey his boss, but he also knows that to do so would endanger an innocent family. As he prepares to leave the store, he sees an advertisement for a cigarette brand in the main part of the pharmacy. The slogan says "ASK DAD. HE KNOWS." That's all the memory jogging George needs. He races to the Bailey Building and Loan office, determined to ask his father what he should do.

While clothed in the wardrobe of humanity, Jesus lived in a culture that esteemed the role of fathers in the lives of their children. First century Jewish fathers understood their God-given responsibility to be life-guides for their sons and daughters. And children knew their parents' wisdom was to be treasured. When children needed counsel or advice, they didn't need to look far. King Solomon's little golden book of wisdom called Proverbs begins with this reminder: "Listen, my son, to your father's instruction and do not forsake your mother's teaching" (1:8).

Fathers were feared, but they were also loved. Children and their fathers enjoyed a special bond. After all, children knew their dads cherished them. Jesus invited us to approach the Almighty and Holy God as a child would come to his father. When teaching the disciples how to pray, he said, "This, then, is how you should pray: Our Father …" (Matthew 6:9). The Aramaic word is *abba* which is very similar to "dada," a baby's first *word* in English. Abba means "papa" or "daddy." It's a child's name for his or her father, filled with intimacy and affection. When we use "Our Father" to address the Creator of the cosmos, we remember how much we matter to God. As a result we express our heart's desires, aware that he wants to hear from us and help us.

Wanting to make sure his disciples knew that their heavenly Father had the same disposition toward them as their earthly fathers, Jesus described the following scenario in Luke, chapter 11:

> *Which of you fathers, if your son asks for a fish, will give him a snake instead? Or if he asks for an egg, will give him a scorpion? If you then, though you are evil, know how to give good gifts to your children, how much more will your Father in heaven give the Holy Spirit to those who ask him!* (vv. 11-13)

In other words, when we find ourselves in need, we need not fear going to our Father in heaven. As trustworthy and kind as most earthly dads are (even those who aren't very religious), he is all the more so. He takes great delight when given the opportunity to show his generous compassion.

When it comes to difficult decisions his children face, our Father is waiting to be consulted. He finds great joy in steering confused kids in the right direction. His only desire is that we come to him with the confidence that he is predisposed to help us. The apostle James is quite clear about that:

> *If any of you lacks wisdom, you should ask God, who gives generously to all without finding fault, and it will be given to you. But when you ask, you must believe and not doubt. (James 1:5-6a)*

Clearly, God loves for us to sincerely ask him for advice. And he definitely knows how to advise us. He is the ultimate example of that Caporal brand cigarette slogan, "Ask Dad. He knows!"

The writer of Psalm 147 puts it this way: "Great is our Lord and mighty in power; his understanding has no limit" (v. 5). Seminary professors have a big, theological word for that kind of all-knowingness: omniscience. Your eight-year-old son might put it this way, "God is a know-it-all!"

When young Isaac went on a camping trip with his father Abraham to Mount Moriah, he knew that they were going to offer a sacrifice to the Lord before eventually heading home. We read about that father-son outing in Genesis 22. Along with their gear, food to eat, and fixin's for the sacrificial fire, the father and son chopped wood for the ceremony. Abraham let Isaac feel the weight of his impending manhood by allowing the boy to carry the wood on his back.

On the day of the sacrifice, young Isaac was perplexed. They had the wood and the fire, but they had left home without a lamb for the burnt offering. Confused, he asked his dad. Abraham simply responded that the Lord would provide. That was all the answer needed to satisfy the boy's inquisitive mind. He turned to his father for advice, and his loving dad did not disappoint him. As it turned out, the boy had nothing to worry about. The Lord did in fact provide.

In the case of young George Bailey, when he arrived at his dad's office at the Building and Loan, he discovered that his father was in the midst of meeting with Mr. Potter. Although George was convinced his dad would help him know what to do with his dilemma, circumstances prevented him from getting a direct answer.

By the time George got back to the drugstore, Mr. Gower was angry that he had not made the delivery to Mrs. Blaine. And even though young George was slapped around before he could explain that the bottle was filled with poison, his bleeding ear was far better than the outcome would have been had he delivered the tainted medicine.

Although Mr. Bailey was not available to answer his son's question at the moment, because George had taken the time to go to his father, a potential disaster was averted. Similarly, when we take the time to go to our Father in heaven with our concerns, we can be assured that he will bring about a positive outcome even if it seems he doesn't hear us at the time (Romans 8:28).

QUESTIONS FOR REFLECTION:

1. When did an employee ask you to do something that placed you in a moral dilemma? What happened?

2. How did your father respond when you asked him for advice in difficult situations?

3. What other Bible verses attest to your heavenly Father's knowledge?

4. Even if you seem to get a busy signal when you call on your heavenly Father, why do you think you should ask him before doing anything else?

Chapter 3

DANCING WITH ADVERSITY

A first glance doesn't always reveal the total picture. That is true of both objects and people. We need to look beneath the surface to see what isn't obvious.

Take the Beverly Hills High School gymnasium as an example. We wouldn't know by looking at the basketball court that a recreational 25-yard long swimming pool is directly beneath the hardwoods. The "swim gym," as it is affectionately called, was designed by Stiles O. Clements and built in 1939. The creative multi-use design was developed in keeping with President Franklin Roosevelt's New Deal.

The scene shot in the Beverly Hills gymnasium is one of the most memorable in *It's a Wonderful Life*. On the night of Harry Bailey's graduation dance, a couple of practical jokers engage the motor that opens the high school basketball court revealing the swimming pool underneath. The unexpected opening of the floor takes place during the Charleston contest. And because the dancers are focused on their footwork, they fail to recognize what looms beneath.

George Bailey and Mary Hatch (the younger sister of his buddy, Marty) are paired up. Their impressive dance steps soon give way to treading water when they accidentally fall in the pool. Dressed in their Sunday best (now soaked), they keep dancing while treading water. They refuse to let their special dance be spoiled after being blindsided by misfortune. Their example of embracing adversity does not go unnoticed. Before long the pool is filled with couples who willingly jump in the water and decide to dance alongside George and Mary. What could have been viewed as a disaster turns out to be the most unforgettable school dance ever.

In fact, the infamous night of the Charleston-in-the-pool disaster will lay a solid foundation of friendship on which George and Mary will build in the future. Four years will pass before George lays eyes on Mary again; but when he does he is ready to take another kind of plunge. The memory they made at the high school graduation dance gives them something tangible to embrace.

Gunder Birkeland learned to dance with adversity. To look at his crippled body, we never would imagine the potential imprisoned inside. As a child in Norway, young Gunder contracted infantile polio. The disease ravaged his body, leaving him a hunchback with twisted feet. He was pulled around in a box like an animal by his siblings. Because of his disabilities and misshapen physique, the neighborhood kids made fun of him. Gunder's parents did not expect him to survive childhood. But he did.

Young Gunder immigrated to America with his four brothers in 1905. Together the siblings worked in a lumber camp. Because of his size and handicap, the normal tasks associated with felling trees took their toll on him. But he refused to let on. When battling homesickness, he persevered. This young, proud immigrant would not let adversity keep him on the sidelines. Instead, he chose to dance with it.

Many thought Gunder was in over his head while trying to stay afloat amid the waves of adversity, but he determined to prove them wrong. What he lacked in physical strength and stature, he made up for with his keen mind. Looking to the Lord for guidance and courage, the young Norwegian leveraged his ingenuity for opportunity, working in the shipyards and investing in rental properties. Eventually Gunder became a successful house builder and investment guru. His obvious limp and physical pain did not keep him off the dance floor. Having learned as a child how to tango with rejection paid off. Letting the Lord lead when he didn't know the steps, taught him trust. His foxtrot of faith would, in time, outfox his critics.

At his death at 90 years old, Gunder Birkeland had outlived all his siblings and died a very wealthy man and a pillar of his church. But if we were to ask him, the man who learned to dance with adversity did not fixate on earthly treasure. Raising three children to love and serve the Lord meant more. His son became a minister and both of his daughters married ministers.

Gunder's experience mirrors the dance steps the apostle Paul discovered firsthand. Paul describes those dance steps in the fifth chapter of his letter to the Christians in Rome:

> Not only so, but we also glory in our sufferings, because we know that suffering produces perseverance; perseverance, character; and character, hope. (Romans 5:3-4)

Falling into unexpected swimming pools need not force us to admit failure and quit. Those problems and trials provide us with opportunities to learn creative ways to continue on. Those "pools" are also situations in which we can discover God's ability to rescue us and carry us to safety. Such trials are the building blocks of character. While others may laugh at our misfortune, the character that eventually climbs out of the water is likely to impress them. Just ask Gunder Birkeland.

QUESTIONS FOR REFLECTION:

1. As you examine your family tree, is there a relative whose experience resembles Gunder Birkeland? What adversity was overcome?

2. Identify some misfortune in your life that appeared to leave you "dead in the water" but from which you eventually benefited?

3. Why do the steps that lead out of the basement of despair (described in Romans 5) form a natural progression? (Problems and trials lead to endurance which leads to character which leads to hope.)

4. Can you make peace with the fact that God at times flips the switch to open the dance floor causing you to fall in the swimming pool?

Chapter 4

Reclaiming 320 Sycamore Street

1600 Pennsylvania Avenue. 10 Downing Street. 30 Rockefeller Plaza. To this list of rather famous street addresses, add one more: 320 Sycamore Street.

The Bedford Falls home of George and Mary Bailey may not compare with the White House, the residence of the British Prime Minister, or the broadcast home of NBC-TV, but it is a place that reminds us of the grace of God.

The Bailey home has its signature mansard roof and classical Victorian design. It was a common home style in the United States from 1855 to 1885. The home at 320 Sycamore Street is known to architecture historians as a "second empire" Victorian. It was a popular style in France in the mid-1800s during the reign of Napoleon III (France's second empire). Thus, the origin of its name. But given what becomes of it in the film, we'd do well to think of the house as a home of second chances.

As we saw in the previous chapter, one of the more memorable scenes in the movie takes place at Harry Bailey's high school graduation party. Even though George has been out of school for a few years, George rediscovers Mary Hatch at this event. The younger sister of George's classmate, Marty, has grown up since the days when George used to serve her sodas at Gower's Drugstore.

Later that night as George is walking Mary home, they pass the old

Granville house at 320 Sycamore. The dilapidated mansion has long been abandoned. For years the windows have been used for target practice by neighborhood boys. It was a myth that if someone made a wish and broke a window, the wish would come true.

Although the frames have few remaining pieces of glass, George picks up a stone to throw it in the direction of the house; but Mary protests. "Oh, no, George, don't. It's full of romance, that old place. I'd like to live in it."

Before launching his well-aimed pebble George counters, "I wouldn't live in it as a ghost."

Not to be outdone, Mary stoops down and throws a pane-smashing stone of her own. When asked about what she had wished for, Mary looks at George with a twinkle in her eye and continues to walk down the street.

Fast-forward four years to George and Mary's wedding day. As the taxi takes them to the train station where they will leave for their honeymoon, they notice a commotion in town. The cause is a run on the bank as well as on the Building and Loan. Without warning, George and Mary's honeymoon plans are put on hold. George leaps out of the cab and races to his office where he spends the day dealing with worried customers. Many of them want their money. At Mary's suggestion, George uses their honeymoon cash to dole out money to customers who demand a withdrawal.

At closing time, George is told that Mary has called and wants him to come home for dinner. But what home? They don't own a house. They were planning to be on a trip. Mary tells him she's at 320 Sycamore.

When George is driven by cab to the old Granville mansion, he is astonished at what he sees. Mary has begun to transform the worthless shell of a house into what will become their permanent home.

Although the house is carpetless and empty, a huge fire is burning in the fireplace. Travel posters decorate the walls. Near the fireplace packing boxes have been stacked together in the shape of a small table. Mary has covered the makeshift table with a checkered oil cloth set for two. A bucket with ice and a champagne bottle sit on the table as well as a bowl of caviar. Two small chickens are roasting over the fire connected to a jimmy-rigged rotating spit. The rig is powered by a string attached to an old-fashioned phonograph playing a record. Mary smiles at her new husband while George can't believe his eyes.

As the newlyweds embrace, Mary admits that this whole scene is what she wished for the night she and George threw stones at the old Granville home. She wanted to live in the place, and she wanted to marry George. While others were content to throw stones at a broken-down building, Mary pictured a beautiful home to which others were blind. Through the eyes of faith, she could see beyond the present.

In the years that follow, Mary remakes that old house. With an investment of love, she gives that run-down worthless building a second life. In a manner of speaking, 320 Sycamore Street is born again. A place despised and ridiculed became a place of warmth and love where the four Bailey children were raised. Once reclaimed, it had a new purpose.

Yes, old buildings can be redeemed. Take the old Enean Theatre in Concord, California. The art deco-style movie house was built in the 1930s. After decades of being a wholesome gathering place for families, it changed its name and its offerings. The Showcase Theatre featured adult films and became known as the local porn palace.

The titillating titles of X-rated features dominated the marquee across the street from where young children played in the park. The Showcase Theatre was a blight on the reputation of a family-friendly community thirty miles east of San Francisco.

The First Presbyterian Church of Concord that shared a back alley with the theatre began to pray about how they might clean up the neighborhood. The pastor and a number of laypersons were convinced that the notorious theatre could be transformed into something wonderful. A successful fundraising campaign resulted in the purchase of the dirty theatre.

But this saga of redemption got a bit muddy as the fine print came into focus. The transaction could only be completed if the existing lease was honored, so the church was put in the undesirable position of being the landlord for the "porn palace." Within a couple of years the lease ran out, allowing the church to do with the building whatever they wished. The result was a beautiful community center conducive for use by various youth organizations, recovery programs, counseling services, and church activities. Not only was the external facade redesigned, the purpose of the building was redeemed to the glory of God.

Gratefully, broken-down buildings that have lost their purpose aren't the only things that are reborn. The Bible is quite clear that the divine architect of our lives delights in designing blueprints that restore and remodel people.

In 2 Chronicles 7:14 the Creator makes his intentions known. Broken lives need not suffer the fate of the wrecking ball: "If my people, who are called by my name, will humble themselves and pray and seek my face and turn from their wicked ways, then I will hear from heaven, and I will forgive their sin and will heal their land."

The Old Testament reads like a catalog of redeemed rascals. Consider the likes of Moses, Miriam, Rahab, Jonah, Samson, Solomon, and Gomer. So does the New Testament: Matthew, Zacchaeus, Mary Magdalene, Nicodemus, and Saul.

In 1 Corinthians 6, Paul reminds professing Christ-followers that willful disobedience has dire consequences. Lifestyles marked by sexual sin, idol worship, adultery, prostitution, or homosexuality will not inherit God's Kingdom. Neither, says Paul, will those who steal, abuse alcohol, abuse people, or cheat others. But then the apostle adds, "And that is what some of you were."

The operative word is *were*. That was their old nature. The old building in which they lived was falling apart and caving in. But that is not the end of the story. Paul continues, "Some of you were once like that. But you were cleansed; you were made holy; you were made right with God by calling on the name of the Lord Jesus Christ and by the Spirit of our God" (1 Corinthians 6:11 NLT). In other words, the potential that God saw in each person was realized.

Paul's description of the redemption process that he has observed in his letters to Corinth is eloquent. Individuals whose lives had been marked by ugly sin have been made over. No wonder the apostle attests to the fact that if anyone is in Christ, he is a new creation. Old things have passed away. Something new has come!

Larry Snydal from Concord, California is a picture of that reality. At forty-five, Larry's abuse of alcohol had cost him his marriage and his job. Without his wife and four daughters, Larry spiraled into the basement of hopelessness. Like the old Granville house, he lacked a sense of meaning or purpose. Without God and without hope, Larry stumbled into a church not far from the converted porn theatre. He confessed his need of a Savior and submitted the blueprints of his future to a heavenly Father he had only heard about. Amazingly, the Lord brought a widowed high school teacher into his life. Linda loved her five kids almost as much as she loved Jesus. After their marriage, Larry and Linda (with her kids) became missionaries with Wycliffe Bible Translators serving in South America. Like George Bailey he was given a new perspective as he looked back on his life. That perspective was called grace. (Coincidently, Larry was a house builder before becoming a Christian and joining Wycliffe. Like the house on Sycamore Street, Larry's "life house" was remodeled, transformed by love.)

QUESTIONS FOR REFLECTION:

1. Think back to when you were a kid. What old building had the reputation of being haunted? How did this reputation impact the way you and your friends acted around it?

2. When you think of a person whose life experienced an "extreme makeover," who comes to mind? What accounted for this "rebirth"?

3. The old Granville mansion was restored due to Mary Bailey. She saw its potential and wouldn't accept that it was beyond renovation. Who believed in your potential and wouldn't give up on you?

4. Who is someone the Lord wants you to "believe in" as a way of bringing about the "makeover" he desires in that person's life?

Chapter 5

BROKEN BANNISTER KNOBS
(AND OTHER BESETTING SINS)

As we saw in the previous chapter, Mary Bailey's ability to refurbish and furnish the old Granville Mansion is no less than amazing. Thanks to her redeeming touch, a broken-down eyesore has become a born-again building. It's a warm, bright, inviting place that symbolizes new life.

But even with all the charm and hospitality, it has one lingering reminder of its past life. The banister knob at the bottom of the stairs remains loose. Time and time again as George Bailey comes home from a long, hard day at the office, the banister cap comes off. It's a perpetual source of frustration for our hero.

All the same, what Frank Capra scripted as comic relief for the film is much more serious when viewed as a snapshot of our life in Christ. Broken banister knobs are a picture of our flawed humanity.

Like the home on 320 Sycamore Street, our old nature has been addressed by grace through faith. We are a new creation. The old has passed; the new has come (2 Corinthians 5:17). Rotten beams have been replaced. Water-damaged carpets have been pulled up. Walls have been moved. The floor plan has been revised. The kitchen has been remodeled. The rodent-infested rafters have been renovated. The overgrown front yard has been newly landscaped. The foundation has passed inspection. We are an extreme makeover big time.

But are we perfect? Do we lack leaks? Are you kidding me? As Paul is quick to admit, our lives of discipleship are works in progress. We are the dwelling place of the Most High God, but we haven't arrived.

In his letter to the church in Philippi, the apostle admits, "Not that I have already obtained all this, or have already arrived at my goal, but I press on to take hold of that for which Christ Jesus took hold of me" (Philippians 3:12).

Did you notice Paul's dual use of the word possess? Christ has possessed him, but he hasn't yet fully possessed the purpose for which the Savior took possession of him. He belongs to Christ, but Christ is still working on certain issues in his life.

In the beginning of Hebrews 12, the writer refers to broken banister knobs in our lives. He writes, "Let us throw off everything that hinders and the sin that so easily entangles."

Dr. Michael Mangis, a psychology professor at Wheaton College, has coined a phrase to describe what theologians historically referred to as our "besetting sin." Mangis refers to the temptations that continually trip us up as "signature sins." These are the patterns of sin in life that are so predictable that these unique temptations seem to bear our name. They are the ways each of us struggle submitting to the Lordship of Christ.

Think of someone you know whose signature sin is pornography. This person probably has battled that demon for a long time. If the person were to chart his or her progress, the graph would likely reveal a series of ups and downs. But not everyone falls prey to images of air-brushed, unclothed models.

Some people we love are tempted by alcohol. Some with whom we attend church are beguiled by prescription meds. The signature sin of many is overeating. Others are tripped up by shading the truth or gossip.

Robert Robinson was only 22 years old in 1757 when he confessed to some signature sin in his life. The evidence is found in a hymn this young Methodist pastor is credited with writing. Robinson's timeless and much-loved "Come Thou Fount of Every Blessing" includes this stanza:

> O to grace how great a debtor daily I'm constrained to be!
> Let Thy goodness, like a fetter, bind my wandering heart to Thee.
> Prone to wander. Lord, I feel it.
> Prone to leave the God I love.
> Here's my heart, Lord. Take and seal it.
> Seal it for thy courts above.

Although we don't know the nature of Robinson's temptation that pulled at him, we do know what it was for Johnny Cash. This music superstar who became a household name in country western music had an open struggle with alcohol and drugs. He started drinking heavily and became addicted to amphetamines and barbiturates in the late fifties.

Unlike Robert Robinson who responded to the grace of God as a young man, the "man in black" was middle-aged before he heard the gospel train a comin'. As a born-again Christian, Cash found inner resources to resist his signature sin for years at a time. But on more than one occasion he lapsed into addiction.

Cash referred to himself as "the biggest sinner of them all" and viewed himself overall as a complicated and contradictory man. But as Johnny Cash stood before tens of thousands at Billy Graham Crusades, the flawed singer gave personal witness to his love of Jesus.

When Johnny Cash died in 2003, his "house" was on a solid foundation, but he still had a broken banister knob. His body was the temple of the Holy Spirit, but the columns had cracks.

Lest we be overly judgmental, we should remember that Johnny Cash and Robert Robinson were not in a league of their own. The household of God is characterized by individuals whose walls are not square.

Eve was easily tripped up by the temptation of wanting what wasn't hers. Abraham had a propensity for lying. Noah battled booze. Moses had an anger issue. Gideon gave into idolatry. Saul was assaulted by ego. David struggled with lust. Solomon was caught in the web of wealth. So was Judas. Peter's signature sin was pride. Martha's was workaholism. Timothy's was fear. Thomas dealt with doubt.

If we're honest, there is a broken banister knob we tend to keep hidden behind the front door. And why shouldn't we be honest? Given those heroes of faith, we're in good company, for sure.

QUESTIONS FOR REFLECTION:

1. What is something in your house that has been on the "fix-it" list for years? Why does it never get repaired?

2. Why do you think the term "signature sins" coined by Professor Mangis is an appropriate description to describe personal temptation?

3. In what ways is the knowledge that the apostle Paul hadn't "arrived" a source of encouragement to you?

4. What is your signature sin? How do you watch yourself so not to fail?

Chapter 6

RESISTING MR. POTTER

Henry F. Potter is bent on controlling Bedford Falls. From his wheelchair, this Scrooge-like Grinch schemes in devious ways to arrive at his self-centered goals. He is not only paralyzed from the waist down, the muscles of his heart seem to lack feeling as well. The latter reality is more tragic than the former.

When Mr. Potter learns that the Bailey Building and Loan is beginning to make inroads into his planned takeover of the town, the old man resorts to an evil ploy. He will try to tempt George Bailey to work for him and in the process, put the Building and Loan out of business.

As the scene in question unfolds, George, seated in Mr. Potter's office at the bank, is offered a cigar. The chair in which George is sitting is rather low and exaggerates the old man's presence as he looks down on him. Potter proceeds to praise George as an outstanding young businessman who is giving him a run for his money (literally).

It is disclosed that George is attempting to make a living and care for his family on an unlikely salary of $45 a week. That's $180 a month or $2,160 a year. Obviously George is overtired, overworked, and underpaid. (In today's dollars George would have made a little more than $30,000 a year.)

Recognizing he has George in a vulnerable spot, the devilish would-be dictator speaks.

> *"I want you to manage my affairs, run my properties,"* Potter exclaims.
> *"George, I'll start you out at twenty thousand dollars a year."* (Likewise,
> *taking inflation and cost of living increases into account since 1946, George*
> *was being offered a salary of roughly $280,000.*)

George drops his cigar on his lap and then nervously brushes off the
sparks from his clothes.

At last gaining his wits, he says, "Twenty thou . . . twenty thousand
dollars a year?"

Potter continues, "You wouldn't mind living in the nicest house in
town, buying your wife a lot of fine clothes, a couple of business trips
to New York a year, maybe once in a while Europe."

George questions how accepting Potter's offer would impact the
Building and Loan. The old man belittles such a question and presses
the young man for an answer. George, obviously tempted by such a
lucrative offer, asks for a day to think about it. Potter agrees to give
him that window of time, and they shake on it.

But as George feels Mr. Potter's cold lifeless hand in his own, he
comes to his senses and recoils with disgust.

> *"No . . . no . . . no . . . no, now wait a minute, here! I don't have to talk to*
> *anybody! I know right now, and the answer is no! NO! Doggone it!*
> *You sit around here and you spin your little webs and you think the*
> *whole world revolves around you and your money. Well, it doesn't, Mr.*
> *Potter! In the . . . in the whole vast configuration of things, I'd say you*
> *were nothing but a scurvy little spider."*

George leaves Potter's office in disgust having resisted a temptation
that could easily have cost him his character and moral virtue.

The temptation in Mr. Potter's office is reminiscent of the scene
screened by the Gospel writers in the New Testament. Following his
baptism in the Jordan River at the hands of his cousin, John, Jesus is
led by the Holy Spirit into the Judean Wilderness. For forty days he
willingly goes without food in order to experience the focused spiritual
insight that accompanies such a fast. And during this season of solitude,
Jesus is drawn into the presence of the Tempter, the devil.

> *Then Jesus was led by the Spirit into the wilderness to be tempted by the devil. After fasting forty days and forty nights, he was hungry. The tempter came to him and said, "If you are the Son of God, tell these stones to become bread."*
>
> *Jesus answered, "It is written: 'Man shall not live on bread alone, but on every word that comes from the mouth of God.'"*
>
> *Then the devil took him to the holy city and had him stand on the highest point of the temple. "If you are the Son of God," he said, "throw yourself down. For it is written: 'He will command his angels concerning you, and they will lift you up in their hands, so that you will not strike your foot against a stone.'"*
>
> *Jesus answered him, "It is also written: 'Do not put the Lord your God to the test.'"*
>
> *Again, the devil took him to a very high mountain and showed him all the kingdoms of the world and their splendor. "All this I will give you," he said, "if you will bow down and worship me."*
>
> *Jesus said to him, "Away from me, Satan! For it is written: 'Worship the Lord your God, and serve him only.'"*
>
> *Then the devil left him, and angels came and attended him. (Matthew 4:1-11)*

Satan knows of Jesus' fast in the brutal heat of the isolated wilderness. So he seizes the occasion and appeals to Jesus' hunger. He tempts the Son of God to turn the sun-baked rocks in the desert into loaves of bread. He tempts Jesus to throw himself off the highest place in the Temple in order to be rescued by angels (more reliable than the one portrayed in *It's a Wonderful Life*). He tempts Jesus to worship him, entitling Christ to own all the kingdoms of the world. All he has to do is sign on the dotted line and go to work for him.

In each instance, the Son of God quotes a passage from Scripture refuting the Tempter's integrity. What George Bailey portrays in the presence of Mr. Potter is what Jesus Christ actually does in the presence of personified evil. As tempting as the "benefits" are, both men recognize the hidden costs associated with such a transaction.

In Peter's first epistle, he cautions Christ-followers to be aware of temptation. This apostle writes from firsthand experience. He failed the temptation-test the night before Jesus' crucifixion. Whereas George Bailey compares Mr. Potter to a spider that traps clueless victims in a web, Peter likens the Tempter to a wild beast intent on consuming its prey.

> Be alert and of sober mind. Your enemy the devil prowls around like a roaring lion looking for someone to devour. Resist him, standing firm in the faith. (1 Peter 5:8-9a)

Peter strongly believes that temptation isn't a threat, it's a given. Satan is moving to trip us up. We have to be listening for near-inaudible paw steps and sensitive to the warm breath of that big, slinking cat. We can't relax in our walk with the Lord. We have to be ready to run. That's what Peter's colleague, Paul, contends. Do you recall what he wrote to his young friend Timothy?

> Flee the evil desires of youth and pursue righteousness, faith, love and peace, along with those who call on the Lord out of a pure heart. (2 Timothy 2:22)

Yes, Mr. Potters appear in every age and in every place but are known by different names. Each one is an ambassador of the devil himself who is deviously intent on derailing disciples who are underpaid, underappreciated, and unaware that he is working overtime to undermine their integrity.

QUESTIONS FOR REFLECTION:

1. Think of someone you know of who lost his or her reputation/ministry/marriage by failing the temptation test. What lessons can you learn from that person's situation?

2. Mr. Potter began his conversation with George by praising his accomplishments. What is it about praise and compliments about which we need to be cautious?

3. Other than Jesus using his knowledge of Scripture to counter Satan's temptations, what else impresses you about this encounter in the wilderness?

4. Peter calls us to stand firm. Paul cautions us to flee. Why do you
   think they suggest different responses? When should you stand firm?
   When should you run?

Chapter 7

When Our Dreams Shatter

The night George and Mary stand in front of the old Granville mansion, they each make a wish before taking turns throwing rocks at the broken window panes. After George shatters glass with his first toss, Mary asks what he wished for. He confidently boasts,

> "Well, not just one wish. A whole hatful, Mary. I know what I'm going to do tomorrow and the next day and the next year and the year after that. I'm shaking the dust of this crummy little town off my feet and I'm going to see the world. Italy, Greece, the Parthenon, the Coliseum. Then I'm coming back here and go to college and see what they know ... and then I'm going to build things. I'm gonna build air fields. I'm gonna build skyscrapers a hundred stories high. I'm gonna build bridges a mile long ..."

George Bailey has his whole life planned. Or so it seems. From the time he was a boy reading travel brochures, he has calculated what he needs to do to see the world and seek his fortune. But as the movie points out, George never leaves Bedford Falls. His dreams are derailed by circumstances that demand more than he has counted on.

In George Bailey we see someone who reminds us of that success-driven person Jesus encountered, the man commonly referred to as "the rich young ruler." That well-known conversation is recorded in Matthew 19:16-22.

A rather self-confident almost cocky individual approaches Jesus and poses a question. "What good thing must I do to get eternal life?" Jesus answers "If you want to enter life, keep the commandments." The man asks which ones, and Jesus answers, "'You shall not murder, you shall not commit adultery, you shall not steal, you shall not give false testimony, honor your father and mother,' and 'love your neighbor as yourself.'"

Obviously quite full of himself, the young man scores his own paper and gives himself 100 percent. But instead of quitting while he is ahead, he presses Jesus with "What do I still lack?" At this point Jesus focuses on the success-driven vision of the man standing two feet from him and demands something that isn't on his five-year plan.

"If you want to be perfect," says Jesus, "go, sell your possessions and give to the poor, and you will have treasure in heaven. Then come, follow me."

The rich young ruler couldn't cash in his blueprint in exchange for Jesus' master plan, however, Rich Stearns was able to.

For Rich Stearns, the American Dream was more than pictures in his subconscious mind while he lay his head on a pillow at night. It was his reality.

Rich grew up in a broken family with an alcoholic father, the son of two parents who never graduated high school. Despite being poor, he went to two Ivy League colleges, earning his BA from Cornell and his MBA from Wharton School of Business. He dreamed of climbing the corporate ladder, and he did. By the time he was thirty-three he had reached a rung that would make most people dizzy. As president of Parker Brothers Games, Rich was more than his first name. It described his status.

In 1995, Rich was named president and chief executive officer of Lenox Inc. As head of the fine china and crystal conglomerate, he oversaw three divisions, six manufacturing facilities, 4,000 employees, and $500 million in annual sales. His salary and bonuses were almost a million dollars a year. He and his wife and five children lived in a ten-bedroom house on five acres outside of Philadelphia.

By his own description, Rich was master of all he surveyed as he looked out from his vast corporate office. He was also a model church-going Christian—a poster boy for successful Christian living.

When an executive headhunter called in 1998, Rich learned that a search was underway for a new president for World Vision International. The man asked if Rich knew of any potential prospects for the position. To Rich, the job description for the head of the Christian relief and development ministry sounded like it was part CEO, part Mother Teresa, and part Indiana Jones. He told the man he didn't know anyone like that. Then the recruiter responded "Well, what about you?"

The question stopped the corporate mogul in his tracks. He knew how to sell luxury goods to the wealthiest people in an affluent nation but didn't know a thing about the poorest of the poor.

When asked if he would be willing to be open to God's will for his life, Rich realized his dreams for his life took second fiddle to the symphony God was orchestrating.

In an interview with Grace Communion International, Rich Stearns recounted his moment of decision. "I was confronted with a stark choice: quit my job, the one I had worked for more than 20 years to attain, take a huge pay cut, sell my house, move my family almost 3,000 miles to a place where we knew no one, and accept a job I didn't want—with a strong likelihood that I would fail and find myself unemployed a year later."

But he took the job, and he didn't fail. He isn't unemployed. Under his leadership, World Vision has achieved a reputation among humanitarian organizations that is nothing short of incredible. If you were to ask Rich to reflect on his life, he would assure you that God's plans are much more fulfilling than the plans he had penciled for himself.

This man who once was president of the company that manufactured "The Game of Life" will readily admit that God's sovereign hand moves us from place to place. We kid ourselves to think life is a random roll of the dice, or drawing a card.

Proverbs 16:9 says "In their hearts humans plan their course, but the

LORD establishes their steps." That same truth is trumpeted by wise King Solomon in Proverbs 19:21. "Many are the plans in a person's heart, but it is the LORD's purpose that prevails."

Like George Bailey, you may think you know where your life is headed. Like the rich young ruler, you may think you know all the answers. Like Rich Stearns, you may think you've reached the pinnacle of success. But what matters more than what you think is what God knows. And he is trustworthy. His plans are good.

> *"For I know the plans I have for you," declares the LORD, "plans to prosper you and not to harm you, plans to give you hope and a future." (Jeremiah 29:11)*

When God shattered Rich's dreams, the glass ceiling at Lenox China and Crystal (of which he wasn't even aware) shattered, too. He was no longer limited to the dimensions of his own dreams. When we surrender to God's will, the sky's the limit.

QUESTIONS FOR REFLECTION:

1. When you were ten years old, what did you dream of doing when you grew up? When you were twenty, how had you revised that dream?

2. George Bailey never reached the pinnacle of success he'd planned, but he was definitely a success in the eyes of the townsfolk in Bedford Falls. Who do you personally know who has a similar story? How has their example impacted you?

3. Rich Stearns was confronted with a choice that required him to redefine success. What is something you feel God calling you to do that others might view as "giving up on the American dream"?

4. Is the sovereignty of God (meaning he gets the final say when it comes to our plans and choices) something for which you are grateful? Why or why not?

Chapter 8

MORE THAN A HOUSE BLESSING

One of the less important, but poignant, scenes in *It's a Wonderful Life* shows the Martini family leaving a miserable shack they have been renting from Mr. Potter and moving into a new home. This is the first home Mr. Martini, his wife Maria, and their four small children have ever owned. Their little cottage is part of Bailey Park, a subdivision of starter homes built by the Bailey Building and Loan Company. It's an initiative George Bailey began that allows young middle class families to purchase instead of rent.

Much like a pastor and his wife caring for their flock, George and Mary Bailey show up to assist the Martinis on move-in day. To help them celebrate this blessed occasion, the Baileys present three gifts along with a blessing for their home.

Mary hands them a loaf and says, "Bread, that this house may never know hunger." She then hands them a box of salt and says, "Salt, that life will always have flavor."

Then George chimes in handing them a bottle, "And wine, that joy and prosperity may reign forever. Enter the Martini castle!"

No direct correlation is made to a spiritual parallel, but Jewish literature suggests that such a house blessing is rooted in biblical faith.

According to the publication "Gates of the House" issued by the Reformed movement of Judaism, bread, salt, and wine were used for the consecration of a Jewish house along with a Bible and a mezuzah (the small ornamented box mounted near the front door jamb in which Scripture portions are contained). The bread and salt symbolize God's provision of adequate food for the home's occupants, while the wine represents God's provision of joy and contentment.

Christian viewers can't help but think of the bread and wine of communion. Standing at the front of the church and offering an invitation to the Lord's Supper, the pastor (like George and Mary) offers a blessing to the household of faith in the name of Jesus. The celebrant of communion is welcoming the family of God to an atmosphere of grace where no one will go hungry or thirsty. The pastor reminds sisters and brothers in Christ that all that is necessary for spiritual nourishment has been provided.

The symbols of Christian communion are the bread and wine of the ancient Jewish feast of Passover. These symbols celebrated God's deliverance of the Israelites from Egyptian bondage during the Exodus. These items called to mind God's provision of food and drink during their sojourn in the wilderness. The Jewish Passover Seder even includes salty water to represent the tears that flowed from 400 years of suffering.

Jesus reinterpreted the meaning of the bread and wine while celebrating the Passover with his disciples the night before he died (Matthew 26:26-29). Breaking the matzo, he likened the unleavened bread to the way his body would be broken by Roman soldiers as they would nail him to a cross. The cup of redemption (the third cup of the traditional Passover meal) Jesus likened to the blood that would flow from his body on the cross. He pictured it as an acceptable blood sacrifice that will result in redeeming God's people. Jesus gave the bread and the wine to his disciples to welcome them into his presence as they crossed the threshold into the Kingdom of God.

Curiously, long before Jesus (or even Moses) instituted bread and wine as appropriate gifts of "welcome" into the household of faith, these two symbols were given to Abram as celebrative gifts. When Abram (who would later be renamed Abraham) was returning home after defeating a coalition of five armies, King Melchizedek of Salem (later to be renamed Jerusalem) approached him. This amazing account is recorded in Genesis 14.

> Then Melchizedek king of Salem brought out bread and wine. He was priest of God Most High, and he blessed Abram, saying, "Blessed be Abram by God Most High, Creator of heaven and earth. And praise be to God Most High, who delivered your enemies into your hand." Then Abram gave him a tenth of everything. (vv. 18-20)

God's provision for Abram and the resultant joy of his victory were appropriately represented by bread and wine. You might say they were symbols of "a wonderful life."

Although the exact origin of the blessing that Frank Capra incorporates into the movie's script is uncertain, it appears to also be a variation of an ancient Russian blessing for newlyweds that reads, "Bread so that you shall never know hunger, salt so that your life will have spice, and wine so your life shall have sweetness."

Jesus also blessed newlyweds with the gift of wine. His first public miracle was at a wedding reception. It is chronicled in John 2 when he took pity on the host's predicament of not having enough wine and proceeded to transform water into wine. It was Jesus' way of blessing the new couple with a sweet send-off and a sense of his supernatural power.

Jesus also made use of bread as he fed his followers in matters of faith. On the hillsides overlooking the Sea of Galilee, he multiplied five small loaves of bread to nourish a large multitude of five thousand people. John chapter 6 tells of Jesus calling himself the bread of life. While being tempted by Satan in the desert, Jesus explained that people cannot live by bread alone but by every word that comes from the mouth of God (Luke 4:4). It's no wonder Jesus' birthplace of Bethlehem is a Hebrew word meaning "house of bread."

And we can't forget salt. That too, was a metaphor of blessing for Jesus. As part of his famous sermon given on the side of a mountain, he told his followers that they were the salt of the earth (Matthew 5:13). In a culture where salt was both a preservative and a flavor enhancer, he blessed his hearers with a powerful word picture. As God's people, their purpose was to preserve a decaying society as well as to season those around them to create a thirst for their heavenly Father.

In addition to the theological implications of bread, salt, and wine in this scene from the movie, the act of the Baileys celebrating with the Martinis also has a spiritual flavor. In Romans 12:15 the apostle Paul reminds us that we are to "rejoice with those who rejoice; mourn with those who mourn."

A Swedish proverb celebrates the truth of this text. "A shared joy is a doubled joy, and a shared sorrow is half a sorrow." In other words, when we come alongside others, we multiply their sense of wonder and minimize the sense of pain.

That means being present with family, friends, and neighbors at meaningful mileposts on life's journey and sharing presents as well.

In the case of a family moving into a new home, our presence and our presents are both appropriate and welcomed. While some may be able to offer six months of a landscaping service as a welcome gift, others can afford to offer bags of groceries to help stock the cupboards, a couple extra-large pizzas for the movers and the family moving in, a guest book to record the visit of subsequent visitors to the new home, paper products (paper towels, toilet paper, napkins, shelf paper, etc.), potted plants, or music CDs of a favorite artist.

You might consider taking your cues from George and Mary Bailey and actually arriving at the doorstep with a loaf of bread, a cylinder of Morton's salt, and a bottle of cabernet (or sparkling cider). Then, as you present each of these symbolic gifts, you could repeat the blessing from the movie. It has been done countless times by those who find this blessing worth repeating.

You may want to give the family moving in an original house blessing. Pastor Reg Simak from Naperville, Illinois did just that. He created this to share as a house blessing with members of his congregation. Because of his love of the house-blessing scene in *It's a Wonderful Life*, Reg included the line "food and drink." He even had his friend Timothy Botts (famed Christian calligrapher from suburban Chicago) render the poem in his creative lettering.

A BLESSING FOR YOUR HOME

Lord, bless this place that, by Your grace,
my friends now call their home.
Please fill it with all that is good and necessary.
Food and drink. Clothing and furnishings.
Art and music. Memories and dreams.
Laughter and love. Health and peace.
Please protect it from theft and fire, earthquake and flood.
Through the clouds of disappointment and loneliness
and sorrow and uncertainty, would You shine Your rays
of hope and confidence and comfort and joy?
And, Lord, may the road that leads to this home
be free from relational potholes and debris.
Let it be an unobstructed path
for those You send to enrich this family's life.
And may the open door of this sanctuary
symbolize their open hearts that long to care
for all who step inside. Amen.

QUESTIONS FOR REFLECTION:

1. What gifts have you given or received on the occasion of move-in day?

2. Why do you think the gifts of bread, wine, and salt were appropriate for the Martini family?

3. If you viewed the communion table at church as the front door to God's House, what significance does the bread and cup have for you as a member of God's family?

4. Reread Pastor Simak's blessing. Now, try your hand at writing a house blessing you could print out and share with the family that has recently moved into your neighborhood.

Chapter 9

Befriending Violet Bick

From the time we first meet Violet Bick in the movie, Capra gives us clues to the fact that her fascination with boys at an early age will likely factor into her future. As we play detective from that point on, we find plenty of fingerprints to dust.

Early in the film, Violet enters Gower's Drugstore and plants herself on a stool at the soda fountain. She refers to the young George Bailey as "Georgie!" She makes sure that the young Mary Hatch (on the stool next to her) knows she likes him.

Mary responds, "You like every boy!"

To which Violet counters, "What's wrong with that?"

Indeed Violet's boy-crazy instincts play out as she grows up. She appears to enjoy the reputation she has developed as a sex kitten. In one scene, as George is about to step into Ernie's taxi for a ride home, Vi walks by and flirts with him calling him "Mr. Bailey."

When George compliments her on her cotton dress, Violet coyly flips her hair and replies "Oh, this old thing? I only wear it when I don't care how I look!" As Vi continues down the street, an elderly man cranes his neck to watch the seductress swivel her hips as he nearly gets hit by a car in the crosswalk.

We catch up to Violet on the night George leaves his brother's wedding reception. Feeling lost and alone emotionally, George walks into town to clear his head. Vi has a guy on each arm in front of a nightclub. Looking into her seductive countenance, we can see the kind of person she has become.

Noticing her childhood friend, Violet engages George in conversation. When she discovers he is headed for the library, she asks, "George, don't you ever get tired of just reading about things?"

George admits that he does tire of living life vicariously and asks Violet if she has plans for the evening. "Are you game, Vi?" George asks longing for companionship. "Let's make a night of it."

"Oh, I'd love it, Georgie," she responds enthusiastically. "What'll we do?"

At that, George waxes eloquently as he describes to Vi the dream date from his point of view. "Let's go out in the fields and take off our shoes and walk through the grass. . . . Then we can go up to the falls. It's beautiful up there in the moonlight, and there's a green pool up there, and we can swim in it. Then we can climb Mt. Bedford, and smell the pines, and watch the sunrise against the peaks, and . . . we'll stay up there the whole night, and everybody'll be talking and there'll be a terrific scandal . . ."

Violet interrupts him: "George, have you gone crazy? Walk in the grass in my bare feet? Why, it's ten miles up to Mount Bedford." When a crowd stops to listen in on this rather unusual conversation, George gives up and tells her to forget the whole thing. Frustrated that Violet's definition of fun is framed by the number of dates she can document during any given week, he walks away.

George has a view of life that is beyond the ordinary. He is aware of joys and experiences for which we were born to which most humans are blind. He knows life is more than sexual fulfillment, courting popularity, or climbing the rungs of success. In George we see a "Christ" figure wanting to introduce his lifelong friend to "the abundant life."

The next time we encounter Violet is in George's office. He has just finished writing something on a sheet of paper and slips it into an envelope. Based on the dialogue that ensues we are led to assume that Violet is about to move to New York City in hopes of rebooting her reputation. George's hand-scrawled note is a letter of reference attesting to his friend's character.

Violet blurts out, "Character? If I had any character, I'd . . ."

George interrupts her and says, "It takes a lot of character to leave your hometown and start all over again."

Although initially resistant to George's offer of some cash he pulls from his pocket, Violet eventually accepts the gift and blurts out, "I'm glad I know you, George Bailey."

Standing on her tiptoes, Violet reaches up and kisses George on the cheek leaving a lipstick smear. As George opens the door to show her out, the office workers focus on the red mark on the boss's face. They can only speculate what had gone on behind the closed door. Curiously, George does not address their raised eyebrows or feel it necessary to explain the lipstick.

It's a noteworthy scene illustrating George Bailey's giving (and forgiving) nature.

Shortly thereafter, we find George panicking over the money that his Uncle Billy has misplaced. When he humbles himself to explain to Mr. Potter his dilemma, the malevolent banker questions George's use of money. He says the word all over town is that he has been giving money to Violet Bick. And George does not deny it.

By not refuting the rumors Mr. Potter alleges, George could be falsely accused of inappropriate behavior with the town slut. But here is a man willing to be wrongly labeled in order to stand up for someone he wants to help.

As we continue to look for God in *It's a Wonderful Life*, we see him in the way George befriends Violet Bick. Isn't his response to her a reflection of the way Jesus dealt with the woman accused of adultery in John, chapter 8?

A woman of the night has been caught in a compromising act and dragged to Jesus in the light of day. With stones in hand the men are ready to kill her in keeping with the Jewish laws. But once again, Jesus proves to be a pebble in their sandals. His response rocks their reality. "Let him who is sinless, toss the ceremonial first pitch!"

Jesus sought out the questionable characters of his day. He hung out with those whom society shut out: tax collectors, prostitutes, drunks, lepers, and Gentiles. No wonder Matthew (a converted tax collector Jesus befriended) nicknamed him a friend of sinners (see Matthew 11:19).

Remember the unnamed woman who anoints Jesus' feet with expensive perfume and then towels them dry with her unbraided hair? Those who witness that incriminating gesture know her reputation and appropriately protest. But Jesus (most assuredly aware of her reputation as well) doesn't flinch. He willingly accepts her token of friendship without concern for their reaction. Let the chips fall (or the lipstick stick) where they may.

How about the Samaritan woman Jesus encounters at Jacob's well (John 4)? At high noon, the rabbi gives her more than just the time of day. And that is a questionable gift. After all, she has been married multiple times and is currently living with a man to whom she is not betrothed.

While she offers him a drink from an artesian spring, Jesus gives her living water drawn from a well that originates in the heart of God. A well she knows nothing about. The conversation they exchanged is far more intimate (and fulfilling) than anything she has ever experienced. Jesus' willingness to befriend her in spite of her sinful ways results in the nameless woman's trust. Because Jesus believes in her, she believes in him. She allows him to help her. In the process, the woman repents and reinvents her life.

That is what we see in the relationship between George Bailey and Violet Bick. We find every indication that George's friendship with Vi and his willingness to believe in her is what leads her to seek him out when she is ready to "repent" and leave town.

A quarter of a century after *It's a Wonderful Life* was released, a musical film was made based on Cervantes's timeless epic *Don Quixote*. In it we have yet another cinematic portrayal of the way Jesus stood up for those society has put down.

The plot is about a middle-aged landowner who imagines himself a knight in armor and goes into the world of the sixteenth century to battle injustice. The movie is titled *The Man of La Mancha*. Watching the engaging film, viewers are not sure if the bearded knight on the tired horse is playing with a full deck. He certainly needs glasses. To him, the windmills he encounters are enemies to be engaged in battle. Foolishly, Don Quixote comes at the rotating blades attempting to joust them. He is a lone lancer who gallops to his own cadence and sees what others cannot.

His abnormal perception is not entirely out of touch with reality, however. In a disheveled and hardened "woman of the night," he sees a prisoner of men's lust, longing to be freed. Her name is Aldonza. But Don Quixote does not see in her what others notice. He sees a beautiful girl with a story yet to be written. He refers to her as "My Lady" and gives her a new name, "Dulcinea." And in one of the more poignant passages in the film, he sings of her new name.

If you cannot see a Christ-figure in Don Quixote, maybe *you* need glasses. No doubt the writer was drawing on his knowledge of Christianity when he wove his plot around the Don and Dulcinea. What a remarkable parallel we find in the life of Jesus and the story by Cervantes and the story about George Bailey. In both stories we can see overtones of Jesus' reaction to the notorious women he befriends. The "self-righteous" see one thing; Jesus sees another. In forgiving them, he renames them. No longer responding to "Guilty" they now gratefully answered to "Forgiven." Jesus loved these ladies, in the truest sense of the word. As a result, he drew out the best in them.

We, too, are called to love the Violet Bicks and Aldonzas in our world. Those others overlook, we are to understand and undergird with friendship. Like George Bailey or Don Quixote or even Jesus himself, we may be slandered for standing up for those "fallen people" among us, but the possibility of redemption is worth it.

QUESTIONS FOR REFLECTION:

1. The screenwriters do not specify why Violet chooses to leave town and start her life over. What do you think might have been the reason?

2. Who is someone you know of whose life was "reinvented" because a Christian friend invested time, acceptance, and grace in his or her life?

3. What are the risks associated with becoming a friend of sinners? What are the rewards?

4. What values or practices do you embrace (based on your relationship with Jesus) that might cause others to accuse you of "fighting windmills" or being "off your nut"?

Chapter 10

"HELP ME, GOD!"

Can't you hear the critics responding to the title of this little book, *Finding God in It's a Wonderful Life*? "Aw, come on! It's not a Christian movie! And besides, how could a sentimental, schmaltzy film like that reference anything theological. You must be kidding! Looking for God in *It's a Wonderful Life*? You don't have a prayer."

Actually, the critics may be right when it comes to that last statement. We don't have just one prayer; we have many. Prayer factors quite significantly into this nonreligious film. And we don't have to look very far to find God showing up. Although we don't see God or hear him, in the opening scene of the movie we hear the voices of people calling out to the Lord while the camera (from an angle over the town) pans over a snowy Bedford Falls.

Mr. Gower the druggist can be heard to say, *"I owe everything to George Bailey. Help him, dear Father."*

Mr. Martini, the owner of the local bar, calls out as best he knows how, pleading to whoever may be listening, *"Joseph, Jesus, and Mary. Help my friend Mr. Bailey."*

George's mother chimes in with, *"Help my son George tonight."*

Bert, the local policeman prays, *"He never thinks about himself, God; that's why he's in trouble."*

Ernie, the taxicab driver adds, *"George is a good guy. Give him a break, God."*

George's wife addresses the Almighty with, *"I love him, dear Lord. Watch over him tonight."*

George's eight-year-old daughter pleads, *"Please, God. Something's the matter with Daddy."*

And finally we hear from the Bailey's youngest daughter, Zuzu, who prays, *"Please bring Daddy back."*

Nearing the turning point in the movie where George meets Clarence, we listen in on a conversation between the wingless angel and Joseph. Before being sent to earth, Clarence is being introduced to the man he is about to help. Joseph explains that during World War II, George was not able to enlist because of being classified 4-F (due to loss of hearing in one ear). Joseph goes on to explain how George spent time in church weeping and praying on V-E Day and V-J Day.

Prayer is also referenced in the film on Christmas Eve, in that tempestuous scene where George loses it in front of his wife and kids. After George leaves the house in despair, Mary dials Uncle Billy. We hear eight-year-old Janie ask her mother if she should pray. Mary immediately replies, "Yes Janie, pray hard." Little Tommy, the Bailey's youngest boy asks if he should join his sister in prayer to which Mary responds, "Yes Tommy, you too!"

But the prayer that most viewers recall in the film is the self-effacing prayer George Bailey offers while seated at the counter in Martini's Bar. He is at his wit's end and completely distraught. The actual screenplay describes the scene in question very succinctly.

> *CAMERA MOVES CLOSER to George. Nick, the bartender, is watching him solicitously. Seated on the other side of George is a burly individual, drinking a glass of beer. George is mumbling:*
>
> *"God... God... Dear Father in Heaven, I'm not a praying man, but if you're up there and you can hear me, show me the way. I'm at the end of my rope. Show me the way, God."*

We can't help but notice to whom the various prayer utterances are addressed: God, Lord, Joseph, Jesus, and Mary. But the one that sticks out is the one here: Father or "Father in Heaven." Here the screenwriter has captured the intimate name Jesus taught his disciples to use when referring to God when he gave them a model prayer in the Gospels. The word in Aramaic is *abba*, which is the affectionate personal name a first century child would use in speaking to his father. The English equivalent would be "papa" or even "daddy."

The references to prayer in *It's a Wonderful Life* are consistent with the role of prayer in orthodox Christianity. Those in need of divine intervention realize they can call out to a merciful, loving Father who (by definition) welcomes his children's cry for help and listens to their pleas.

In the bar scene, Frank Capra celebrates the authenticity of a simple prayer offered by a nonreligious person recognizing his sincere need of God. George Bailey admits to not being a religious person. But with that disclaimer, he calls out to God, aware he is not deserving of that for which he seeks.

That's the very picture of authentic prayer Jesus sketches in his parable of the Pharisee and the tax collector in Luke 18:

> *To some who were confident of their own righteousness and looked down on everyone else, Jesus told this parable: "Two men went up to the temple to pray, one a Pharisee and the other a tax collector. The Pharisee stood by himself and prayed: 'God, I thank you that I am not like other people—robbers, evildoers, adulterers—or even like this tax collector. I fast twice a week and give a tenth of all I get.' But the tax collector stood at a distance. He would not even look up to heaven, but beat his breast and said, 'God, have mercy on me, a sinner.'*
>
> *"I tell you that this man, rather than the other, went home justified before God. For all those who exalt themselves will be humbled, and those who humble themselves will be exalted." (vv. 9-14)*

This parable elevates the humble person aware of his sin and humbles the person who has elevated himself into thinking that he has The Book of Common Prayer memorized. Notice Jesus' fondness of the tax collector. When we own our guilt and unworthiness, we at once are forgiven and are made worthy.

In this parable, Jesus denounces prayer that is characterized by flowery, high-brow phrases and offered by self-righteous self-focused pray-ers. It was against the background of repetitive mindless rituals that Jesus introduced his disciples to a more authentic way of praying which he modeled in the Lord's Prayer. Remember his warning?

> *When you pray, do not keep on babbling like pagans, for they think they will be heard because of their many words. (Matthew 6:7)*

The kind of prayer that pleases the Lord is family talk arising out of the moment of awareness and need—not as a pipe organ or keyboard belches in the background, but through everyday life.

By the way, did you know that during the prayer scene in Martini's Bar, a secular Italian love song can be heard sung as a duet? The woman's part is sung by Adriana Caselotti who did the singing and speaking parts for *Snow White* in the 1937 animated Disney classic. You can actually see Adriana standing behind Jimmy Stewart in the scene.

By his own description, the prayer scene was Stewart's favorite in the entire film. As a professing follower of Jesus Christ, Stewart personally resonated with the script he was asked to render. He understood the power of prayer.

In a 1977 article in *Guideposts* magazine, Stewart wrote, "As I said those words, I felt the loneliness and hopelessness of people who had nowhere to turn, and my eyes filled with tears. I broke down sobbing. This was not planned at all, but the power of that prayer, the realization that our Father in heaven is there to help the hopeless had reduced me to tears."

For director Frank Capra, the non-churchy nature of the prayer scene gave it believability. "It's a short prayer, but we believe it. [George is] desperate and has nowhere to turn. If we showed him on his knees or in a private corner the audience wouldn't take it in. But in a bar right after gulping down a shot of whiskey, we are inclined to believe it" (Frank Capra Interview edited by Leland Poague, 2004, University Press of Mississippi).

Sadly, for many Bible-believing Christians, prayer has lost its earthiness. It has become the realm of memorized mantras or ornamented rituals. We need to be reminded that prayer in the New Testament, for the most part, is not reserved for synagogue or temple. It is the gutsy, conversational utterance that is rooted in real need and honest communication.

- Peter, sinking in the stormy waves, prays, "Lord, save me!"

- The thief on the cross, measuring his ebbing strength and fleeting breath, prays, "Remember me when you come into your kingdom."

- The father of the demon-possessed boy prays, "I do believe; help me overcome my unbelief!"

- Even Jesus models a non-stained-glass-posture when he prays, "My Father, if it is possible, may this cup be taken from me."

- Paul, the reluctant apostle, when bucked from his high horse prays, "Who are you, Lord?"

- John the elder, while exiled on an island in the Mediterranean, prays, "Amen. Come, Lord Jesus."

The view of prayer we see in the movie is the same view Paul invites us to consider in Philippians 4:6:

> Do not be anxious about anything, but in every situation, by prayer and petition, with thanksgiving, present your requests to God.

It is the immediate unrehearsed plea of one who is talking to someone they know loves them. They know because this someone has demonstrated time and time again how much he (in fact) does.

QUESTIONS FOR REFLECTION:

1. On what occasions was prayer practiced in your home when you were a child?

2. Why is prayer best understood as the communication between a child and a loving parent?

3. The prayer scene in Martini's Bar illustrates Jesus' parable of the Pharisee and the tax collector. Describe a situation when you have witnessed the attractive authenticity of a nonreligious person reaching out to God.

4. What steps can you take to improve your prayer life?

Chapter 11

WHEN GOD SENDS ANGELS
INSTEAD OF MONEY

You've no doubt heard the expression, "God always answers prayer; sometimes he answers with yes, sometimes with no, and sometimes with wait."

But he always answers. Unlike some friends who can't be trusted to respond to voice mail or texts, the Almighty doesn't disregard our inquiries. He takes them seriously.

And he responds compassionately. Jesus took special effort to make sure we could peek into the Father's heart when it comes to prayer. And the image he made sure we'd see is that of a loving father who responds appropriately and with care: "Which of you, if your son asks for bread, will give him a stone?" (Matthew 7:9).

But at times, God's answers aren't immediately obvious. He answers in a loving way; but we don't recognize the circumstances as God's answer until after the fact.

George Bailey discovered that. In Martini's Bar he calls out to the Lord in desperation and asks for help. As George leaves the lounge, he steps out into a heavy snowfall and proceeds to drive his car into a tree. Leaving his car, he trudges through the deepening snow to the bridge at the edge of town.

On the bridge George leans up against the railing and attempts to gather up enough courage to jump. Having convinced himself that he is more valuable to his family dead than alive, he prepares to plunge to his death.

At that very moment, George sees a person struggling in the icy river. The unidentified individual flounders, unable to swim. Instinctively, George jumps from the bridge but with a different purpose. Instead of dying in a pool of self-pity, George puts himself aside to save another. He dives to rescue a person we soon discover is Clarence Oddbody, AS2.

As the "Angel Second Class" and George dry off in the bridge tender's office, the two engage in conversation about how God answers prayer. George bemoans the fact that after calling out to God for help in Martini's Bar, a man busted him in the jaw. Some answer to prayer, George scoffs. To which Clarence counters that *he* is the answer to George's prayer.

By feigning drowning, Clarence diverted George from following through on his suicide attempt. Instead of drowning, George "saved" Clarence. By putting himself in the position of needing to be rescued, Clarence had in fact saved George's life.

When George prayed for divine intervention at Martini's Bar, he wasn't exactly sure for what he was praying. Most likely he assumed his problems would be solved by God supernaturally providing him money to cover the missing funds. After all, the shortfall of $8,000 is what had caused George to spin out of control from his cruising altitude.

But God knew better. The Lord knew that George was about to kill himself. From God's point of view, "help" for George meant helping to keep him alive. That's why Clarence was dispatched. To save the despondent husband and father's life was an immediate answer to George's prayer for help.

What follows in the movie illustrates an even more complete answer to George's plea for assistance. George doesn't need money as much as he needs to know how wealthy he already is because of the investments he has made in the lives of his family, friends, and neighbors. So God's ultimate answer to prayer provides George with a renewed love of life by giving him a chance to see all he had taken for granted.

The answer to prayer was different than George expected but an answer nonetheless.

In 1947, a year after *It's a Wonderful Life* debuted, Hollywood released another movie that featured an angel dispatched from heaven in answer to a cry for help. *The Bishop's Wife* starred David Niven, Loretta Young, and Cary Grant. (Karolyn Grimes also stars in *The Bishop's Wife*. She plays the Bishop's daughter, Debbie, in the film. Karolyn is the one who played George and Mary Bailey's daughter, Zuzu, in *It's a Wonderful Life*.)

In *The Bishop's Wife*, The Reverend Henry Brougham (played by David Niven) is attempting to raise money for the construction of a multi-million dollar cathedral. Having recently been promoted from parish priest in a poorer part of the city to esteemed bishop, Henry is overwhelmed by his new responsibilities.

Early in the film, we find Henry standing in front of a large fireplace in his home office. An artistic rendering of the future cathedral hangs above the mantel. We hear him pray, "*Dear God —what am I to do? Help me...!*"

As in *It's a Wonderful Life*, God's answer to prayer does not come as expected. No windfall amount of money is forthcoming. Rather an angel (played by Cary Grant) arrives on the scene to calibrate Henry's perspective. The angelic visitor succeeds in helping the bishop navigate the treacherous trail of ministry that is booby-trapped by ego, fame, and the tendency to please people.

Henry Brougham's prayer for guidance is indeed answered. But the way the answer is packaged and delivered initially sets Henry back on his heels.

Indirect answers to prayer are more than recipes that make for tasty plots on the silver screen. They are the stuff out of which biblical truths are illustrated. God's Word is filled with examples of divine answers showing up in disguise.

Do you remember the story in 1 Kings 17 when Elijah prayed for food? God's answer was unexpected and perhaps initially unrecognized.

He sent a flock of ravens. The ravens in turn delivered the nourishment the prophet needed.

David prayed for permission to build a temple to replace the tabernacle that housed the Ark of the Covenant. More than anything else (except maybe for writing psalms), David wanted to honor the Lord by constructing a permanent place of worship. He did get an answer, but it wasn't what he had expected. God made clear to King David that the temple would be built but by his son Solomon (2 Samuel 7).

The prophet Daniel prayed for God's will in his life as well as for God's people exiled in Babylon. The answer was not what Daniel expected. He was imprisoned in a cave inhabited by lions to prove God's presence and protection in his life (Daniel 6).

Do you not recall that the nation of Israel prayed for a military ruler? The Messiah of their dreams was a conquering war hero. But God answered their prayers by sending a "man of suffering," "familiar with pain," a disfigured emissary from whom they hid their faces (Isaiah 53).

In John 11, we read about Mary and Martha praying that their brother Lazarus will be healed. The Lord answered their prayer by letting him die so that God's power over death could be revealed. As a result of that power, Lazarus was resurrected to life.

Acts 3 introduces us to a crippled man whose daily practice was to sit at one of the gates of the Jerusalem temple and beg. His prayer (if the truth were known) was for money. Much like the homeless we encounter who hold up handmade signs and camp out at street corners and off-ramps, begging was this man's primary means of income. So as Peter and John passed the crippled beggar, he wondered if God would answer his prayer for money. Would these two men be prompted by God to give him a handful of coins? Well, God did answer his prayer but not as he had expected. Through Peter and John the man was healed. He prayed for money but was healed instead.

In Mark 2, we read about the friends who creatively transported their paralyzed friend to where Jesus was, even though that meant tearing a hole in the roof of another person's home. Their prayer was for their friend to be restored to health. Imagine their shock (and disappointment) when Jesus responded to their prayer with "your sins are forgiven." A spiritual healing wasn't what he had been praying for, but apparently it was what he most needed.

The paralytic eventually got his physical healing as well, but that doesn't always happen. Take the apostle Paul, for example. The apostle prayed that a chronic physical malady from which he had suffered for years might be healed. God answered, but not with a healing. God's unexpected answer was to provide Paul with the grace he needed to endure what he would continue to suffer (2 Corinthians 12).

As these examples from Scripture point out, God's answers to our prayers aren't always what we have in mind. Contemporary songwriter Laura Story knows all about that.

In 2004, Christian recording artist Chris Tomlin recorded a song written by Laura. "Indescribable" would become the number one worship song of the year. Her career as a songwriter took off. Life was good! She went on to marry her handsome, athletic fiancé Martin. In 2006, however, Martin was diagnosed with a brain tumor. During surgery to remove the tumor, he contracted meningitis. Having experienced the blessings that came from writing a worship chorus about the indescribable nature of God, Laura now prayed for blessings amid the indescribable suffering of her husband's illness. Breathing machines and post-op memory and vision loss was unimaginable for this newlywed couple.

Prayers for healing did not result in total recovery. But opportunities to minister to countless individuals dealing with sorrow and suffering have emerged through Laura's music and Martin's experience. It was against the backdrop of their personal heartache that Laura wrote a song celebrating God's answers to prayer that are other than what we expect.

In her song "Blessings," she references the way we routinely ask the Lord for peace and protection and call on him for comfort. Her lyrics uncover how we tend to interpret hardships that blindside us in spite of our prayers. We doubt God's goodness and in anger question his presence. We grow bitter when friends betray us or circumstances suck us dry.

But then the songwriter begins to ask a series of questions that confront those of us who pray with the distinct possibility that the trials God allows in our lives are his mercies in disguise. That we tend to lean on God more when there is less of our own resources on which to draw. And if that is the case, God is not guilty of not being good or not being near. He is only guilty of answering our prayers in ways that are different than we hoped.

QUESTIONS FOR REFLECTION:

1. When did you attempt to throw a pity party for yourself but were interrupted by someone whose trials were more disastrous than yours? What did you do?

2. In both *The Bishop's Wife* and *It's a Wonderful Life*, the most significant need is not money but change of perspective. Why do you think it often takes a sense of "poverty" to hear God speak?

3. With which biblical example of camouflaged answered prayers do you most identify? Why?

4. Looking back, describe a time in your life when your trials were actually God's mercies in disguise.

Chapter 12

How Do You Spell HALLELUJAH?

George finds himself in desperate straits on Christmas Eve. While his wife and children are busy with preparations for the families to gather at their home, George is paralyzed by fear. The likelihood of prison (due to the missing $8,000) has catapulted him into panic mode.

As George returns home from the office he hears "Hark the Herald Angels Sing" coming from the family's upright piano. His eight-year-old daughter, Janie, is practicing in anticipation of a carol sing later that night. But her uneven pounding of the keys (and missing some sharps) compounds her father's consternation with which he entered the home. So does son Pete's inquiry for help as he works on a Christmas reading for the family gathering. When Pete asks how frankincense and hallelujah are spelled, George erupts with "What do you think I am—a dictionary?"

George's sarcastic and insensitive retort is painful to watch. We grieve for little Pete. All the same we can likely empathize with this frantic father. When our world is crashing down, we bite the hand of one we love much like an injured dog resists the well-intentioned stroke of its master.

As we watch George implode, he throws an uncharacteristic adult tantrum. Exploding, he tips over a table as all the contents go flying. He loathes the fact he has so many kids and complains about their drafty home. He's upset the doctor was called to examine a younger daughter sick in bed. Everything seems wrong.

And when everything is going south, finding true north on our spiritual compass can be difficult. Even Christ-followers find Christ-like responses difficult at times—especially when we are questioning how to make sense of life's confusing circumstances. When the presence (or purpose) of God isn't obvious, we strike out in uncharacteristic ways.

Hallelujah can be difficult to spell (let alone say it) when we are backed against the ropes and sense a knockout punch is inevitable. The apostle Peter illustrates that tendency. After vowing unconditional loyalty to Jesus at the dinner table earlier in the evening, the fisherman-turned-disciple curses out an innocent servant girl who asks if he is a friend of Jesus. Having witnessed his rabbi's arrest in the Garden of Gethsemane, Peter's world is falling apart.

He appears to have no way out. The one on whom he had pinned his hopes is about to be tortured and executed. Peter dances with his despair and then loses control, striking out.

During the holidays, we can find spelling hallelujah with the letters of our life to be very challenging indeed. The imperfections of life are magnified this time of the year. So are our expectations, not to mention our expenses. While the "Hallelujah Chorus" plays, its message is often lost. Hallelujah isn't even in our dictionary.

We may sing "Hark the Herald Angels Sing" but can barely hear them over the shouting of an adolescent child or the inconsolable crying of a diapered infant. At Christmastime, the recent death of a child, parent, or broken marriage creates pain in such piles that it dwarfs the mound of presents beneath the tree.

You might not be missing $8,000, but like George Bailey (or Peter) you can't bring yourself to say hallelujah—let alone spell it. But this very season celebrates the fact that God entered into our world to experience our despair and stress firsthand. The Incarnation is the Creator's way of walking a mile in our moccasins. Because he came to us (in Jesus) as one of us, we have the confidence of knowing we are not alone in our despair. Even more amazing, our Savior is acquainted with our grief and is in a position to lift us out of the basement of helplessness.

Because of Christmas, we have the means of praising God in all circumstances. We can voice a hallelujah in the midst of trying times. The next time you find yourself trying to spell "hallelujah," use the following acrostic. It is based on George Bailey's experiences after storming out of the family home driven by fear and frustration.

H = *humble yourself before the Lord.* After humbling himself and going to Mr. Potter for help, George discovers that he is worth more dead than alive. It's a devastating realization. From Potter's office, George heads to Martini's Bar where he sits at the counter and comes to terms with the fact that he cannot solve the problem he is facing. This is this point where he humbles himself before the Lord as well.

James reminds us that if we humble ourselves in the eyes of the Lord then he will lift us up (James 4:10). We can't assume a posture of praise until we have mounted off of our high horse. Our heavenly Father longs for us to kneel in his presence.

A = *admit your need.* Having humbled himself, George goes on to acknowledge that he needs help. He is willing to own up to the fact that he has problems in his life. This man who had been in charge of most everything in his life cannot control what is going on around him. And he admits it. Paul says we are strong when we admit to being weak. For in our weakness, God's strength is most visible (2 Corinthians 12:9).

The apostle also makes it clear that we are to have an honest estimation of ourselves instead of pretending to be what we aren't (Romans 12:3). The Greeks of the first century had a word for pretending: hypocrite.

L = *look to God.* Though he was sitting at the bar in front of an empty glass, George knows that the answer to his dilemma is not in a whiskey bottle. He wrings his hands and looks up calling on divine help. It's as if he knows the Scripture that claims those who call on the name of the Lord shall be saved (Romans 10:13).

L = *lose yourself in another's need.* From Martini's, George heads to the nearby bridge where he isn't sure he wants to live any longer.

While contemplating jumping to take his own life, he sees someone floundering in the river. George jumps to save the person's life. And once he helps Clarence stay afloat and reach shore, he has been diverted from his self-destructive mission. Taking his eyes off his own problem is the next step in discovering the solution that has eluded him.

Didn't Jesus call us to deny ourselves, take up our cross, and follow him? (See Matthew 16:24.) Didn't he also say, "Greater love has no one than this: to lay down one's life for one's friends"? (See John 15:13.) Didn't Paul call us to bear one another's burdens? (See Galatians 6:2.)

E = *evaluate your circumstances.* Once Clarence the angel hears George wish that he had never been born, he decides to give him a taste of an alternative reality in which he is granted his desire. In this setting, George is given the means of looking at his problem from a new perspective.

That's what happened to Jonah. When he was convinced he knew what was going on in his life, the Lord provided him a change of venue. And in the belly of a big fish, the struggling prophet could evaluate God's purposes for his life.

L = *list your blessings.* Once George has evaluated his situation from a new perspective, he is in a position to take stock of his blessings. As George discovers how dark and deplorable the world is without having benefited from his influence, he realizes what a wonderful life he actually has. He is reminded how he cherishes his wife and kids, his home, his business, his neighbors, and his friends.

In Psalm 90, Moses advises us to number our days that we might gain a heart of wisdom. Adding up our blessings is a great way to do Moses' brand of math. When we list the "goods" we've been given, we are less apt to fixate on the bad stuff that is part of every human life. Listing our blessings is actually a form of giving God praise.

U = *unconditionally embrace today.* Having come to terms with just how blessed he is, George asks the Lord for the privilege of living life again. He realizes that not being born is not all that great. And when he is given the chance to "live again," he gains a spring in his step and vitality to his voice. He runs through the town of Bedford Falls greeting everything and everyone, including the malevolent Mr. Potter. As imperfect things are, George sees them as a gift.

The Bible speaks of our life as a gift to be unwrapped and enjoyed. Paul cautions the Christians in Ephesus to make the most of each opportunity. Such intentionality is a sign of being wise as well as being filled with the Holy Spirit. (See Ephesians 5:15-19.)

J = *joyfully celebrate!* After running through Bedford Falls in a one-man celebration parade, George makes his way home to 320 Sycamore Street. He bounds into the entryway smiling from ear to ear with hugs for everyone. Here is a man who has renewed capability of recognizing the treasures his life contains. He still has hurdles to leap, but they do not define his future. There is music! There is wine! There is laughter and singing.

A realigned perspective of life complete with a renewed sense of gratitude results in a positive perspective on life. A joyful life (much like a grateful life) is a tangible expression of praise to God. In Isaiah 55:12, we read the connection between joy and praise. "You will go out in joy and be led forth in peace; the mountains and hills will burst into song before you, and all the trees of the field will clap their hands." By definition, when we are joyful, worship happens.

A = *acknowledge Divine intervention.* The movie concludes in the shadow of the Bailey Christmas tree with George reunited with his wife Mary, and holding his little daughter Zuzu in his arms. George looks in the basket of contributions collected from generous neighbors and friends and discovers a copy of *The Adventures of Tom Sawyer.* Opening the cover of the book, he reads an inscription from Clarence the angel. It is all the proof George needs that he has been the recipient of heavenly help.

Authentic worship consists in giving credit where credit is due. The psalmist was quick to cue the ancient choir of Israel. "Praise the LORD, my soul, and forget not all his benefits" (Psalm 103:2). We are called to acknowledge the faithfulness of our heavenly Father whose mercies are new every morning (Lamentations 3:23).

H = *hear the music of heaven.* In the final scene George is infused with a sense of wonder. Surrounded by those who love him, he joins in singing praise to God with the lyrics of a familiar carol. Harry offers a toast to his brother George "the richest man in town." Everyone sings "Auld Lange Syne." Then a little bell tinkles on the Christmas tree. Zuzu, cradled in George's arms, says, "Teacher says every time a bell rings, an angel gets its wings." George looks heavenward and winks. In the ringing of the little bell, he has heard the music of heaven. And having heard it, George at last has learned how to spell "HALLELUJAH."

Our praise of God is not complete until we listen with our hearts to what the Holy Spirit is attempting to communicate to us. Once again it is the psalmist who advises us to "be still, and know" God's presence (Psalm 46:10).

QUESTIONS FOR REFLECTION:

1. George is quite sarcastic when his son asks for help in spelling Hallelujah. Identify a time when you have taken out your frustration on a family member. How did you eventually smooth things out?

2. Why do you think the Christmas season magnifies the anxiety and stress that leads to depression and suicide attempts?

3. The Bible says we are to give thanks *in* all things not *for* all things (1 Thessalonians 5:18). What do you think is the difference?

4. Which of the points in the acronym for hallelujah spoke the most directly to you? What will you do to spell "hallelujah" in your life?

Chapter 13

YOU CAN'T HAVE A MERRY CHRISTMAS WITHOUT MARY

Marley was dead to begin with. There is no doubt about that . . .

With those familiar words Charles Dickens begins his timeless novel *A Christmas Carol*. The author tells his readers that on Christmas Eve of 1843, Jacob Marley, the business partner of Ebenezer Scrooge, died in London. Also on Christmas Eve, exactly seven years later, the wealthy miser is given a peek at his spiritual poverty while being escorted through a surrealistic journey of his life. No wingless angel for Scrooge. The ghosts of Christmas past, present, and future are his guides.

On this less-than-merry Christmas Eve, Scrooge comes face-to-face with the pitiful prospect of his personal world—a world devoid of the faith, hope, and love that was birthed in the world when a young virgin by the name of Mary had a baby in Bethlehem. What he sees is deplorable. He is beside himself with angst. Christmas may be here, but it is anything but a merry one for Scrooge. There is no doubt about that.

Similarly in *It's a Wonderful Life*, Christmas Eve is when George reaches the end of his rope. The decorated Christmas tree in the Bailey living room and the sounds of Christmas carols from the family piano cannot awaken the spirit of the season within George. Even his son's request for help spelling "hallelujah" evokes a humbug reply.

As George leaves the Bailey home in utter frustration, Mary recognizes that her husband is in trouble. She dials Bedford 2-4-7 and reaches George's Uncle Billy. She soon discovers the dilemma causing her loving, Bob Cratchet-like husband to act more like Ebenezer Scrooge. The Building and Loan has misplaced $8,000 in cash with the bank examiner due to arrive. (While $8,000 may not appear to be a lot, in today's dollars that would be over a million dollars.)

Mary is willing to do whatever she can to be a means of grace in rectifying the seemingly hopeless situation. She wastes no time conceiving a plan that will birth hope. She goes through the town explaining the situation and calling on family, friends, and neighbors to contribute to the "George Bailey salvation" fund.

Those who hear of the need respond generously. Even the Bailey maid, Annie, who has been hoping and saving for a husband, offers the contents of her special account. Mr. Martini breaks open the jukebox at his bar and contributes all the coins. Mr. Gower gives Mary all he has collected from drugstore customers who had unpaid invoices. Even Violet Bick gives the money George had given her for her flight to New York City because of a change in her plans. Mary's college boyfriend and entrepreneur, Sam Wainwright, learns of the dilemma and sends a telegraph authorizing a loan of up to $25,000.

When George finally returns home from Clarence the angel's guided tour of Pottersville, he is welcomed with the news that Mary has saved the day. Her labor of love has brought joy to their world. There is no doubt about that.

According to the Gospels of Matthew and Luke, that is what Mary the mother of Jesus did as well. She made herself available as a vessel into which the wine of redemption could be poured. When confronted with God's plan for humankind by the angel Gabriel who then explained her part in the plan, she willingly said, "Let it be!" Without Mary we would have no Merry Christmas!

Ironically, the majority of evangelical Christians fail to embrace the significance of Mary in the Christmas story. The shepherds get their rightful due. The angels arouse our curiosity. We focus a spotlight on the Magi. Even the innkeeper is awarded reward points (even though the Bible mentions no such person). But without the teenage girl who made herself available to the Holy Spirit, we would have no Christmas.

Some believe that certain expressions of Christianity overemphasize Mary, but she remains a model of virtue and obedience. Listen to her unrehearsed hymn of praise recorded in Luke 1.

> And Mary said: "My soul glorifies the Lord and my spirit rejoices in God my Savior, for he has been mindful of the humble state of his servant. From now on all generations will call me blessed, for the Mighty One has done great things for me—holy is his name. His mercy extends to those who fear him, from generation to generation. He has performed mighty deeds with his arm; he has scattered those who are proud in their inmost thoughts. He has brought down rulers from their thrones but has lifted up the humble. He has filled the hungry with good things but has sent the rich away empty." (vv. 46-53)

Mary did what was asked of her out of a heart of love and devotion. That's what another Mary did. This Mary met a successful surgeon while working as a nurse. She and Don married. Together they raised six sons. Because of their doctor-dad's hectic schedule, the majority of the parenting responsibilities fell on Mary. Chauffeuring the boys to school commitments, sports activities, and church functions kept her busy.

Mary believed in her sons, regularly communicated her love of them to them, and prayed for their future pursuits. Tragically, one of the boys was seriously injured in an accident that cost him his vision. Mary drew from her training as a nurse as she spent countless hours caring for her son for the better part of a year.

When her doctor husband grew disenchanted with the marriage and left, Mary did what circumstances demanded and redoubled her efforts to hold the family together. This was most noticeable at Christmastime when Mary created a festive atmosphere complete with foods, traditions, and music from her Danish heritage.

Amazingly, Mary's selfless investment in her sons paid off. One is a doctor, two are lawyers, and three have made their mark in the business world.

All three Marys were willing to respond to unanticipated circumstances and do what was asked of them. But they are not the only ones who are called to lives of love, devotion, and service. All servants of Christ are. When we recognize that we have been placed by God in a situation to address what is wrong, we have no choice but to "be like Mary." Like the precious girl who carried Jesus (full-term) into our world, we, too, have the privilege of carrying him wherever we go.

One contemporary hymn writer put it this way:

> We carry Christ to others through our friendship.
> A listening ear, a hand that reaches out.
> Making the time to get to know our neighbors.
> Discovering their passions, fears, and doubts.
> Extending mercy when their hearts are broken.
> Transparently acknowledging our pain.

By the end of Dickens's *A Christmas Carol*, Ebenezer Scrooge had become that kind of friend. His "humbug" had become a "hallelujah!" He had discovered Mary's secret to experiencing a Merry Christmas. There is no doubt about that!

QUESTIONS FOR REFLECTION:

1. In the church today, why do you think Mary is often deprived of the honor she deserves?

2. When you were a child, who in your life was most responsible for your Christmases being "merry"? Why?

3. In the cases of Mary Bailey, the Virgin Mary and Mary, the doctor's wife, each succeeded in doing what the circumstances dictated. When did you fail in a critical situation? When did you come through, like Mary Bailey?

Chapter 14

FINDING ZUZU'S PETALS

In the 1994 remake of the movie *Little Women*, tragedy strikes when Beth succumbs to a contagious illness. Hannah, the March family servant, is seen spreading rose petals over the vacated bed. These flower fragments are a tangible symbol of death even as they attempt to fill the empty room with a fragrance of life.

In *It's a Wonderful Life*, flower petals are also used as a prop. But in the case of the Capra plot, Zuzu's petals are symbolic of life and love.

Zuzu, the Bailey's youngest daughter, is in bed with a bad cold. She was given a flower as a prize at school earlier in the day. So Zuzu walked home without buttoning her winter coat, not wanting to crush her flower. But exposure to the elements apparently took its toll. She has a temperature of 99.6 degrees.

One of the most poignant moments in *It's a Wonderful Life* is the touching scene where George Bailey sits on the edge of the bed and comforts his little girl. Although his temper had flared to fever pitch just moments earlier downstairs, George cools off in order to engage Zuzu in conversation.

Zuzu shows her dad her prized plant. When he offers to "give the flower a drink," Zuzu resists, wanting to get out of bed and do it herself. A few of the wilted petals fall off; she is horrified and asks her father to paste them back on.

George turns aside so his daughter can't see and then tucks the orphaned petals in the watch pocket of his trousers. He hands the flower back to Zuzu appearing to be good as new. Before leaving her room, George tenderly invites his daughter to go to sleep and dream of her flower becoming a colorful garden. She willingly complies.

Later that night as George is granted his wish of never having been born, he reaches in his pocket for Zuzu's petals only to discover they aren't there. Clarence reminds him that if he had never been born, neither would Zuzu. Thus he would not have had an experience that would result in her flower or its petals.

But when George reaches the point where he prays, "I want to live again!" and he awakens from his nightmare, he discovers the petals are in his pocket after all. Those few little flower petals are tangible reminders of his wonderful life and a family that loves him.

In the drama of redemption, the storyline of faith is filled with symbols. They are tangible items that connote a spiritual concept. Just think about it.

Apple
Olive branch
Rainbow
Staff
Serpent on a pole
Ark of the Covenant
Golden calf
Fire
Cloud
Scarlet thread
Lamp
Gold, frankincense, myrrh
Five stones and a slingshot
Five loaves and two fish
Roman coin
Perfume
Bread and wine
Basin and towel
Cross
Empty tomb

But there is a specific visual aid which stands out in the Old Testament as a symbol of God's faithfulness, something that is akin to Zuzu's petals.

After God disciplined his people for their disobedience with a forty-year "timeout," the Israelites finally crossed the Jordan River into the Promised Land. Joshua gave the following instructions to the elders of Israel.

> Joshua called together the twelve men he had appointed from the Israelites, one from each tribe, and said to them, "Go over before the ark of the LORD your God into the middle of the Jordan. Each of you is to take up a stone on his shoulder, according to the number of the tribes of the Israelites, to serve as a sign among you. In the future, when your children ask you, 'What do these stones mean?' tell them that the flow of the Jordan was cut off before the ark of the covenant of the LORD. When it crossed the Jordan, the waters of the Jordan were cut off. These stones are to be a memorial to the people of Israel forever." (Joshua 4:4-7)

The pile of stones became an inaudible rock concert of sorts for the succeeding generations. As they saw their grandparents' collection piled high on the banks of the river, they would be prompted to ask the significance. And the questions would provide an opportunity for the older members of the family to recount stories that spoke of God's provision and punishment as well as his mercy and faithfulness.

Another often overlooked symbol is found in 1 Samuel 21:1-9. When David is fleeing for his life from the bipolar king of Israel, he seeks the help of a priest. The fugitive shepherd-turned-court-musician is hungry and vulnerable. He asks the priest for food. All that is available is the sacramental bread, symbolically displayed on the sacred table. The priest offers this "consecrated bread" to David.

When the future king inquires about available weapons with which he can defend himself on the run, the priest offers him a sword that is wrapped in a blanket in a closet. When David learns that the available lance is actually the "sword of Goliath," he gratefully accepts it replying, "There is none like it."

Why would David say such a thing? The sword was not his. It had belonged to the nine foot tall gargantuan from Gath. Ah, but herein is the reason behind David's remark. The sword of Goliath had Zuzu's petals-like qualities.

David had taken down the Philistine giant with a sling several years before. When the teenage shepherd accomplished what none of Israel's brave soldiers could, everyone knew that God had intervened on behalf of his people. David approached the unconscious champion and severed his head with the defeated enemy's weapon.

The sword of Goliath symbolized victory. It spoke of God's faithfulness. As David held the sword in his hand, the cold, metal handle awakened faith. He was reminded of his wonderful life. Much more than a weapon of protection, the sword of Goliath was a visual aid that prompted David's memory of God's deliverance.

We all need visual aids that jog our memory. We are prone to spiritual dementia and require tangible items that trigger what we tend to forget. As George Bailey fingered the loose petals in his watch pocket, he felt all the proof he needed to realize that all would be well. So, we too, need something to touch or see that dwarfs our doubt and feeds our faith.

Maybe it's a baptismal certificate signed by your parents' pastor and folded in your baby book. Perhaps it's that Gideon New Testament you received as a fifth grader that symbolizes your commitment to Christ as a child. It could be a teacup and saucer you inherited from a godly great-aunt who prayed for you as you went off to college. It may also be the hospital identification bracelet you wore when doctors thought you were going to die, but God had other plans. Maybe it's a miniature wooden cross left anonymously in an Easter basket at your front door (along with money-filled plastic eggs) on the Good Friday you were laid off from your job.

You probably have a number of objects tucked away in a scrapbook, drawer, or closet that remind you how God came through for you. Why not bring them out of hiding and allow them to fill your home with the refreshing fragrance of Zuzu's petals?

QUESTIONS FOR REFLECTION:

1. Will Ackerman is an acoustical guitarist and recording artist who created a record label called Windham Hill. He recently wrote a song

called "Zuzu's Petals." What is it about the symbol in George Bailey's pocket that has such a lasting legacy in popular culture?

2. Create a rock collection similar to the one described in Joshua 4. What twelve milestones in your life can you identify that speak of a spiritual lesson? Form a pile of small polished rocks of differing colors that represent those twelve events. Keep the pile in a prominent place in your home or office.

3. George's solution to Zuzu's problem wasn't what she had in mind. He "fixed the flower" by putting the fallen petals in his pocket. Although God never fools us, he sometimes answers our requests differently than we thought he might. When has that happened to you?

4. What tangible symbol do you plan to display that will be a constant reminder of God's ability to care for you?

Chapter 15

There's a George Bailey in Each of Us

One of the reasons *It's a Wonderful Life* is the favorite movie of countless people is because so many identify with the main character. George was just an average sort of guy with a desire to embrace life fully. He wasn't especially bright. He had ordinary looks. He didn't come from a wealthy home. He probably lacked the coordination to excel in high school sports. But he loved people and unwrapped each day as a gift to be enjoyed.

If you've seen the film, you know George Bailey was the oldest son of Peter Bailey, the owner of the Bailey Brothers Building and Loan Association in Bedford Falls, New York. He was a conscientious boy who earned his parents' trust. As a twelve-year-old, George rescued his little brother Harry from a life-threatening sledding accident. He learned responsibility working as a soda jerk and delivery boy at Gower's Drugstore. His good-natured personality and community involvement won him a lot of friends.

In the scene where George works at Gower's Pharmacy, his passion for life is as easily detected as is his skill as a soda jerk. Those who swivel on the stools in front of him may order their favorite fountain creation, but George is the one who orchestrates the conversation. He flavors the atmosphere like he adds flavor to the malts.

George was a dreamer. He loved putting shredded coconut on ice cream sundaes because it reminded him of the South Pacific where coconuts grew. The sound of trains rolling through town fueled within him an inbred wanderlust. He probably hung travel posters on his bedroom walls so that he would be more apt to experience those far-off places while he drifted off to sleep.

But George's dreams were not limited to visiting exotic cities. He dreamed of making something of himself.

The Bible refers to that kind of mark-making drive as being made in the image of God. Alive to life. Genesis 1:27 says, "God created mankind in his own image, in the image of God he created them; male and female he created them."

What separates human beings from the animal kingdom is our ability to reflect on our abilities, contemplate the God who gave them to us, and find ways to employ them as a way of leaving our mark in our world.

Teachers leave marks on students. Artists leave marks on canvas. Poets leave marks on paper. Photographers leave marks on film. Sculptors leave marks on metal. Writers leave marks on their readers.

Because we are made in the image of God, we have an insatiable desire to create. We have within us the desire to make our mark. And all because God has left his mark in us. We see that desire in George Bailey, the dreamer. From the time he was a kid, he had dreams of traveling the world and making it a better place. He wanted to "*build things, design new buildings and plan modern cities.*"

George pictured a better world. He envisioned a peaceful place where families like the one in which he grew up could taste the sweet nectar of life marked by health, housing, education, safety, freedom of worship, and friendship.

George saw through the empty life of a dollar-driven Mr. Potter. He realized even as a young boy, that the hated bank president of Bedford Falls had created a less-than-wonderful life for himself. George dreamed of proving to Mr. Potter and everybody else in town that we have another way to dance with the opportunities God places in our path.

There's a little bit of George Bailey in all of us. We all dream of making a difference and making our lives count. As we watch George relate to his peers, his parents, and his friends, we feel as though we are looking in a mirror. We, too, want to do what it takes to stand up for what is right and expose what is wrong.

That God-given instinct to dream big and make a difference is what motivates men and women to run for public office. It's what explains how successful executives leave profitable companies to volunteer in a third-world country. It's the reason college graduates turn down well-paying suburban school jobs in order to work with Teach for America in a struggling urban district.

The Bible introduces us to a young dreamer named Joseph. We meet him in Genesis chapter 37. Joseph dreamed big. He had eyes to see a world in which he would play a significant role in bringing about the plans the Creator had lined out in His Divine Blueprints. Joseph's father and brothers made fun of his dreams. They failed to see what their younger brother visualized.

Another Joseph captured the dreams of the Joseph in the Bible lyrically. Some fifty years ago Joe Darion wrote a song for the musical *Man of La Mancha*. It's a lyric that provides a vocabulary for everyone in touch with their God-given passion to change their world.

To dream the impossible dream . . .
To fight the unbeatable foe . . .
To bear with unbearable sorrow . . .
To run where the brave dare not go . . .
To right the unrightable wrong . . .
To love pure and chaste from afar . . .
To try when your arms are too weary . . .
To reach the unreachable star . . .

This is my quest, to follow that star . . .
No matter how hopeless, no matter how far . . .
To fight for the right, without question or pause . . .
To be willing to march into Hell, for a heavenly cause . . .

Heavenly causes may seem out of this world and out of our reach. But dreams to change the world begin by making a difference in our own sphere of influence. George Bailey's dream began while working for Mr. Gower in the local drugstore.

Several centuries before Joe Darion wrote "The Impossible Dream," a monk, who loved animals almost as much as he loved God, verbalized his George Bailey instinct in a prayer. We call it the Prayer of St. Francis. It too, captures the essence of our dreams. Way back in the thirteenth century he dreamed of being a conduit of God's grace in the world. For Francis the dream was possible if he made himself available to the Lord in ordinary ways every day.

Taking up his pen he inked a sheet of parchment with these words:

> Lord, make me an instrument of your peace.
> Where there is hatred, let me sow love.
> Where there is injury, pardon.
> Where there is doubt, faith.
> Where there is despair, hope.
> Where there is darkness, light.
> Where there is sadness, joy.
> O Divine Master,
> grant that I may not so much seek to be consoled, as to console;
> to be understood, as to understand;
> to be loved, as to love.
> For it is in giving that we receive.
> It is in pardoning that we are pardoned,
> and it is in dying that we are born to Eternal Life.
> Amen.

And a person doesn't have to be a saint to live out the prayer of St. Francis. It's the privilege of every person ever born. The George Baileys of our world as well as the Pam Higgins-es.

Pam Higgins hails from Wenatchee, Washington and easily relates to George Bailey. Day after day, she stands behind the counter at the Owl Soda Fountain serving up sundaes, ice cream cones, and shakes. Those who frequent the local sweet spot can attest to the Bailey-like attitude toward life they see in Pam. It's a can-do spirit that characterizes the community in which she grew up. You might even call it a counterculture.

In 2002, the Owl Drugstore closed due to larger supermarkets moving into the area. For Pam, who had worked at the pharmacy since high school, the closing meant a loss of a career. For the community, who had depended on the drugstore's soda fountain for more than a century, it meant the loss of a landmark.

With dreams of finding a way to keep the fountain from closing, Pam and her husband, Frank, found a way to borrow money from the bank and move the marble counter, red padded stools, and all the equipment two blocks down Main Street. This middle-aged mom didn't want to let the customers down. And the risk paid off; her dream of keeping the landmark from closing came true.

Today, the Owl Soda Fountain continues to be a gathering place in the Wenatchee Valley. It's a place where business merchants, shoppers, and students take a meaningful break during the day to refresh their thirsts and renew their confidence that dreams really can come true. God intended them to.

QUESTIONS FOR REFLECTION:

1. George wanted a big suitcase on which to apply stickers from all the far-away places he would one day visit. Where have you had the privilege of traveling overseas? What was your favorite place? Why?

2. What does being created in "the image of God" mean to you?

3. George Bailey dreamed of making a difference with his life. As a child, what did you dream of doing with your life?

4. How do you relate to George Bailey? What dreams do you feel God has planted in your heart today?

Chapter 16

SUFFERING WHEN IT'S NOT YOUR FAULT

George Bailey had big dreams for himself and his family. He had big dreams for his business and for the clients of Bailey Building and Loan. As a kind and decent man, George settled for smaller personal dreams in order to help those in need reach theirs. His kind and caring attitude prompted him to delay his college education to take over the family business when his father died. It prompted him to forgo his honeymoon when the needs of his depositors took precedence over the celebration of his marriage to Mary.

His kind character also resulted in George experiencing undeserved suffering. As a boy working in Gower's Drugstore, George is whistling behind the counter. Mr. Gower calls out from the background "You're not paid to be a canary." His speech is slurred and uncharacteristic. George notices a telegram near the cash register indicating that Mr. Gower's son has died of influenza at the university.

Retreating to the back room, George finds his boss inebriated and upset. As he observes Mr. Gower attempting to fill a prescription, he realizes something is wrong. The medication being put in the pill bottle is poison. George disobeys his boss's order to deliver the medication. When Mr. Gower discovers the disobedient behavior, the drunken pharmacist forcefully hits his young employee, slapping George's bad ear with an open palm. When George explains why he couldn't do what he was asked, Mr. Gower discovers his mistake. In spite of the apology,

George suffers for doing the right thing. But that's not the only time this kind and decent fellow is caused to suffer for another's actions.

When Uncle Billy, the absentminded brother of his deceased father, misplaces the Building and Loan's deposit of $8,000, George is the undeserving victim. With the state bank examiner scheduled for an audit, he is held responsible for the missing funds. This unexpected (and undeserved) complication in George's life is what carries him to the brink of despair.

George doesn't deserve to be the victim of his Uncle Billy's absentmindedness. But he is. Is it fair? Absolutely not! But then again, when was fairness ever a guaranteed outcome? Experiencing a bad outcome through no fault of our own is called suffering. It's called welcome to life.

Who hasn't been blindsided by misfortune and questioned life's meaning? Who hasn't asked questions such as, Why do the innocent suffer? Or where is God when justice is held hostage?

That's the premise of the book of Job. A righteous man was buffeted by heartbreaking tragedies even though he didn't do anything to warrant them. His so-called friends couldn't imagine a world in which bad things happen to good people. Job's cadre of critics attempted to squeeze him for some confession of transgression. But Job refused to play their game. He knew he was suffering blamelessly. For some reason the Almighty had allowed him to lose his family, his home, his business, and his health.

Throughout the book of Job we are reminded that life in a broken world includes hardship and heartache. It also includes the presence of God who will bring good from bad in his good time. The story of Job concludes similarly to *It's a Wonderful Life*. A windfall of blessing more than compensates for that which was lost.

We see that same scenario in the biography of Abraham's great-grandson. Joseph is the "George Bailey" in the first book of the Bible. He not only dreamed big, he also suffered unjustly. From the time he was a boy clothed in his colorful coat, this young son of Jacob had visions of greatness.

In his dreams, he pictured his older brothers and father bowing down and honoring him because of his accomplishments. But those brothers, jealous of their visionary sibling, sold him to a caravan of traders headed to Egypt. Faking their brother's death, they lied to their father saying he was killed by a wild animal.

Upon reaching Egypt, Joseph landed a job working for Pharaoh's captain of the guard. This conscientious employee earned his boss's trust. But he was falsely accused of raping the man's wife. For two years "the dreamer" was unjustly jailed. He helped a couple of fellow inmates understand troubling dreams. One promised to tell Pharaoh about his abilities when he was released, but forgot. Joseph's suffering in prison continued until he, at last, was invited by Pharaoh to interpret *his* dreams. At that point, Joseph was appointed by the king of Egypt to be second in command of the whole realm.

Ironically, the injustice (and cruel) behavior of his brothers accounted for an unanticipated blessing. Because Joseph was sold into slavery, he ended up in Egypt and ultimately in a place of unique influence. Because of the unjust suffering he endured, Joseph was in a position to provide his family food when they traveled to Egypt during an intense season of famine. Joseph's suffering was redeemed in due time. Joseph allowed the people of God the means to stay alive when it seemed they were doomed to die out.

The story of how a young shepherd boy, David, became Israel's most famous king also tells how suffering gave way to blessing. Most people know the story of how he distinguished himself as a kid worthy of a crown. He leveled Goliath with one well-aimed stone rocketed from his slingshot. Not as many recall that he had been anointed king by the prophet Samuel only after David's brothers had been passed over as unqualified. But fewer still know "the wonderful life" sequence that resulted in David and his brothers even being born.

It all goes back to the story recorded in the Old Testament book of Ruth. A man by the name of Elimelech had a wife and two sons. They lived in that little town called Bethlehem a few miles outside of Jerusalem. During a season of extreme drought and famine, Eli pondered his options. He was a farmer and could make no money on his land. So he made a difficult decision.

Packing up his wife Naomi, and his sons, Mahlon and Kilion, Eli moved to the Gentile nation of Moab, east of the Jordan River. There he settled, established a new home and friendships, and began to work the land. His sons grew up and married. But then Eli became sick and died. This is a tragic turn of events for Naomi, but before long, tragedy struck again: both her sons succumbed to death.

Naomi was left alone with her two daughters-in-law in a foreign country separated from her relatives to the west. She decided to return to a more familiar setting and released her sons' widows from any obligation to move with her. But Ruth insisted on accompanying her mother-in-law.

Upon returning to Bethlehem, Naomi introduced her daughter-in-law to a wealthy farmer who was a distant relative of her late husband. Boaz provided an income opportunity for Ruth and later married her. Even though he was significantly older than Ruth, Boaz's bride became pregnant and had a baby boy named Obed. When Obed grew up and married, his wife gave birth to a boy named Jesse. And when Jesse became a husband, his wife gave birth to several children. The lastborn of the kids was a boy they named David.

Now, isn't that amazing? Had Eli never moved his family to Moab, Israel would have an entirely different history. Had Ruth accepted Naomi's offer to stay in Moab, she never would have married Boaz. And despite the suffering and heartache associated with the story of Ruth, we see a good outcome. All things did work together for good!

From the Bible and our own experiences we are forced to admit that suffering finds our street number and knocks on our front door. Someone has rightly stated that we are either just coming out of a season of struggle, in the midst of one, or about to enter into one. Karolyn Grimes would certainly agree.

Like George Bailey, Karolyn had big dreams. Her childhood dreams were fed by early successes only to be derailed by setbacks over which she had no control.

Karolyn, as a child actor, played George Bailey's daughter Zuzu in the movie. She was only six years old at the time. The following year she landed the part of Debbie in *The Bishop's Wife*. Like the fictional life of George Bailey, Karolyn's early life was marked by happiness and big dreams. The adorable performer seemed to have staked a claim in the golden land of movie studios.

By the time Karolyn was fourteen, sorrow showed up demanding a screen test. Her mother died of early-onset Alzheimer's disease. A year later, her dad was killed in a car accident. Authorities placed Karolyn with an uncle in Missouri.

Her uncle's wife was not happy having her live in her home, so the transition was quite painful for Karolyn. She had lost both of her parents, been uprooted from a career and community she loved, and placed in a family that didn't want her.

Ironically, the events that led George Bailey to thoughts of suicide in *It's a Wonderful Life* were nothing compared to the not-so-wonderful pain and heartache that parked outside Karolyn's home.

Karolyn determined she would not cave in. Recalling Bible verses she had learned as a little girl in Sunday school, she claimed the truth of Psalm 23: "The Lord is my shepherd. I shall not want . . ." Karolyn pictured the Shepherd caring for her in the presence of her enemies and found her identity in the school choir and drama club.

While pursuing a degree in music, she met a young man who offered her the security she had not found in her surrogate family. They were married and had two daughters. But after less than ten years, the marriage collapsed.

Karolyn worked as a medical technician to provide a living for her growing children. Two years after her husband left, he was killed in a hunting accident, leaving the girls without a daddy. Despite the divorce, his death impacted her in significant ways.

She knew she needed someone in her life to help raise her girls. And soon she fell in love with a guy who had three kids of his own. It was like a Brady Bunch marriage. In addition to the handful they brought to the relationship, they had more to call their own.

Once again, however, the marriage proved difficult. Karolyn poured herself into raising her kids, while her husband pursued his own career. When their 18-year-old son committed suicide a month before his high school graduation, the stress on the marriage resulted in a lengthy separation and her husband's eventual death to cancer.

In her early fifties, Karolyn wondered where God was in the suffering he'd allowed in her life. She knew he was there somewhere. Her extensive collection of crosses that hung in her home were a constant reminder that suffering is at the heart of the faith she professed.

About this time, a renewed interest in *It's a Wonderful Life* caught on across the country. An unintended lapse in renewing the movie's license resulted in it being shown on cable television outlets throughout the Christmas season. Target stores featured miniature Christmas village figurines and buildings. Gift books about the movie were published.

To Karolyn's delight, requests for personal appearances began to pour in. People wanted to hear her story. They were interested in what it was like playing Zuzu, but they were also curious about what had become of her life when Zuzu's petals had blown away.

Karolyn Grimes was given a great gift. For the next twenty years, she was able to cobble an income and travel the country by talking about her not-so-wonderful life that had become quite wonderful after all.

QUESTIONS FOR REFLECTION:

1. Identify a time in your life when another person's choices caused hardship for you. How did it affect your relationship with that person?

2. Why do you think God allows suffering in the lives of those who are seeking to please him?

3. Joseph told his brothers "What you intended for evil God intended for good!" Describe a time when personal hardship in your life resulted in something positive that you couldn't have anticipated.

4. How will knowing the not-so-wonderful life of Karolyn Grimes affect the way you watch *It's a Wonderful Life* the next time you see it?

Chapter 17

WHAT IF YOU HAD NEVER BEEN BORN?

Have you ever taken the time to ponder what would have happened if you had never been born? I recently did.

I found a letter that my maternal grandfather had written two years before I was born. In the brief note, my mother's father requested family members to pray for a decision his son was about to make. Ben, a pastor near Seattle, was considering the possibility of moving to Northern Idaho to a larger congregation. Papa Birkeland wanted the Lord's will to be done.

My uncle decided to accept the call to the church in Lewiston. There he met a young Greek American bachelor pastor who he introduced to his unmarried baby sister. After thirteen dates they were married. Fifteen months later I was born.

As I read my grandfather's letter, I realized that my uncle could have easily stayed at his church. Had he done so, I never would have been born.

My friend Dave can relate. His mom was accepted at Wheaton College but couldn't afford to go. After working two years, she enrolled at the University of Illinois. In the meantime, Dave's dad had begun his studies at Wheaton but left after two years, transferring to the University of Illinois to study engineering. While they could have met at Wheaton as eighteen year olds, they didn't. Instead, while both were studying in Champaign, a traveling evangelist (who knew each of them from different contexts) introduced them to each other.

Had Torrey Johnson never introduced them, Dave's parents never would have been married, and he never would have been born.

If you examine your own story, you will likely see how a change of plans or change of dates would have altered the way your personal history played out. Everyone can attest to the way circumstances intersect and affect the lives of other people.

Just how one life touches another is the central theme of *It's a Wonderful Life*. About three-quarters of the way through the film, George Bailey is so overwhelmed with a sense of hopelessness, he verbalizes his despair claiming the world would be a better place without him. Inside the bridge tender's office, George and the wingless angel begin a conversation, and the movie takes a turn.

> *"I supposed it would have been better if I'd never been born at all," George sighs.*
> *"What'd you say?" Clarence the angel asks.*
> *George repeats his earlier admission. "I said I wish I'd never been born."*
> *"Oh, you mustn't say things like that," the angel says gently rebuking George. But adds, "Wait a minute. That's an idea."*

Clarence rubs his chin as his eyes light up. It occurs to him that when a person imagines what the world would be like without him or her, the person gains a fresh appreciation for how blessed a life he or she really has. Clarence realizes that George's true worth will resurface once he begins to understand how much his life has contributed to others.

So Clarence begins to shepherd his new friend through a world deprived of George Bailey. The result is a dark, hopeless community. Bedford Falls no longer exists. The city limits sign indicates they have entered Pottersville. The reason? Mr. Potter has looked out for his own interests (financial gain at any cost) and built a community on a foundation without morals. The wholesome tree-lined village of shops and family-friendly parks has been replaced by flashing neon signs marking a seedy collection of taverns, gambling halls, and jazz clubs.

Gower Drugstore is no more because Mr. Gower went to prison for poisoning a child. That's because George wasn't there to call attention to the life-threatening error the grief-stricken pharmacist was making due to lack of judgment upon learning by telegram of his son's death.

A troop transport is sunk because Harry Bailey never grew up to fly anti-aircraft missions in the war. That is because Harry died at the age of nine since he didn't have an older brother who could have saved his life in the sledding accident.

Billy Bailey went to prison for his inability to account for missing funds at the Building and Loan because George was not able to take responsibility for his uncle's absentmindedness.

Mary Hatch never became Mary Bailey because George was never a part of her life. Sadly, she never married at all and lived a dreary, lonely life.

Through it all, George Bailey concludes that his life, although complicated by financial woes, was nonetheless very worthwhile. Had he never been born, the lives of countless people would have been deprived of a wonderful life. The difference one life makes is incalculable.

But because George Bailey *was* born, he grew up to save his younger brother from drowning (which allowed Harry to become a fighter pilot and save countless troops on a transport). George *did* keep Mr. Gower from making a tragic decision that would have poisoned a child and sent the druggist to prison. He delayed going to college to run the family business and kept it from going under. With the encouragement and support of his wife Mary, George went on to establish Bailey Park, a housing development affordable to young families.

Any fan of *It's a Wonderful Life* can't imagine a world without George Bailey any more than followers of Jesus can consider a world without Moses!

According to the book of Exodus, such a world is not all that far-fetched. Pharaoh issued an edict demanding that all male babies born to Hebrew slaves be killed. This gender-specific infanticide was the rule of the land. It was ignored at the risk of death.

But Jochebed, Moses' mother, was convinced her newborn baby boy was special. Deep in her heart she believed the God of Abraham, Isaac, and Jacob had a unique purpose for his life. As a result, she was willing to take a chance and disobey Pharaoh's dictate. For three months, she hid her child in her home. But the baby begins to grow, making it increasingly difficult to keep her secret, so she weaves a floating basket of reeds and places her son in a shallow eddy of the river.

When one of Pharaoh's daughters discovers the baby in the basket, the Egyptian princess lays claim to the child. She names him Moses, which means "to draw out" because she drew him out of the water. Moses' sister, who has been watching on behalf of their mother, emerges from a nearby hiding place and she offers to find someone who can nurse the baby. Amazingly, the princess agrees and even pays Jochebed for doing the very thing the mother thought she would never be able to do again.

This person whom God would use to draw his people out of slavery and out of Egypt almost perished as a baby. Given the circumstances at the time, Moses never should have survived.

Just imagine how the history of God's people would be different if that little Hebrew boy had been drowned at birth. They would have had no deliverer. The Hebrews would have remained slaves laboring under the North African sun, building pyramids. They wouldn't have been able to escape Pharaoh's tyranny. There would have been no Passover. No parting of the Red Sea. No promised land flowing with milk and honey. No Ten Commandments.

Moses may have had his own "George Bailey moment" in the course of his forty-year trek across the Sinai wilderness. When humbled by the chronic complaining and godless rebellion of the Israelites, Moses likely rued the day he was born. Can't you see Moses thinking that the world would have been a better place without him?

But God had a better plan. One man was the key to so much of Israel's development. Without him, the awe-inspiring story of biblical faith (embraced by Jews and Christians alike) would be nonexistent.

In the eighth chapter of Romans, the apostle Paul celebrates God's ability to weave the circumstances of our lives together. The result is a quilted tapestry that displays his glory, beautifies the world, and brings the meaning of our lives in focus. One life intersects countless others.

And we know that in all things God works for the good of those who love him,
who have been called according to his purpose. (Romans 8:28)

But this is not only true in the Bible or a classic Christmas movie. The intersecting threads in the tapestry of history cannot be ignored. One life is intricately connected to the lives of other people. Those you influence actually end up influencing others.

Take Hugh Steven's life for instance. Hugh was conceived by an unmarried teenager in Canada. His mother could easily have terminated the pregnancy. This was not a legal practice, but it wasn't unheard of either in 1931. But she carried the baby to term. She attempted to care for her son for six months but then decided to give the child up to the Children's Aid Society.

For nearly three years, little Hugh was passed from foster home to foster home. His sickly nature conspired against the provision of a stable family situation. At last a couple, unable to have children of their own, took him in. As part of the agreement with the agency, they promised to provide religious instruction for the child. When he reached school age, Hugh was dropped off at Ruth Morton Baptist Church. His parents didn't attend, but they made sure their son went to Sunday school.

Hugh took a keen interest in what he heard on Sunday mornings. In time, he accepted Christ as his personal Savior. Through the youth group at church, Hugh met the woman who would become his wife. Together they responded to an invitation to serve as career missionaries with Wycliffe Bible Translators.

Hugh began researching and writing the back stories related to Bible translation and resultant conversions. Over the span of fifty years, he wrote more than thirty books (many published in several languages). Hugh and his wife had four children who were nurtured in biblical values. Two married pastors. Another went as a Bible translator to Indonesia and another went to work for a Christian parachurch ministry. Their offspring also include three teachers, three professional musicians, a professional basketball player, an artist, an international lawyer, and a Christian counselor. Had Hugh's mother aborted him, no lives would have been impacted by his books and the lives of his children and grandchildren would not have existed.

Several years ago, Hugh had the opportunity to meet his half-siblings (born to his birth mother in Canada) and their spouses. But he discovered a sobering fact. None of them had any knowledge or interest in the Christian faith. It was as though he had been plucked out of an irreligious setting and placed in a situation where he would hear God's voice and follow God's plan.

Hugh's amazing story illustrates that each life is part of God's perfect plan. Every person is essential to bringing about his purpose in history. The prophet Jeremiah was convinced of this. In the first chapter of his Old Testament prophecy, he records the words of the Creator that reveal the value of an individual life:

> *Before I formed you in the womb I knew you, before you were born I set you apart; I appointed you as a prophet to the nations. (Jeremiah 1:5)*

But, even if you're not a prophet to the nations, you are a person with a holy purpose. From the time God first thought of you and pictured you on planet earth, he has choreographed your steps and orchestrated your circumstances in order to positively impact people in your sphere of influence. Even before you were conceived by your parents, your heavenly Father conceived in his mind how you would waltz with wins and tango with losses. And in each situation, others in your life would be inextricably shaped by your presence in theirs.

The writer of Psalm 139 poetically described how the fingerprints of the Creator are easily seen in the process that brought our lives into being:

> *For you created my inmost being; you knit me together in my mother's womb. I praise you because I am fearfully and wonderfully made; your works are wonderful, I know that full well. My frame was not hidden from you when*

I was made in the secret place, when I was woven together in the depths of the earth. Your eyes saw my unformed body; all the days ordained for me were written in your book before one of them came to be. (vv. 13-16)

Because God was involved in the decision that you would be born, believe he is still actively involved in it. Never minimize the importance of your life. Remember when Clarence the angel was dispatched from heaven by Franklin and Joseph? He was told that someone on earth was about to throw away God's greatest gift. And what was that gift? It was human life. Yours included.

QUESTIONS FOR REFLECTION:

1. Dust for fingerprints in your own personal story. What seemingly "random" events resulted in your parents getting together? What circumstances might have prevented you from being born?

2. Identify someone who has impacted your faith in a significant way. How would your life be different if that person had never been born or died in infancy?

3. Who are five people you have influenced through your friendship, faith, job, or volunteer efforts? Try and list the names of those they have influenced.

4. How has your life been touched by someone taking his or her own life? What lasting impact has that suicide had on you and others?

Chapter 18

WHAT IF JESUS HAD NEVER BEEN BORN?

December, 1943. The United States had just concluded its second year engaged in World War II. Heartsick mothers somberly anticipated vacant seats at the family dinner table on Christmas Day. Patriotic fathers prayed for the safe return of sons from the frontlines. Confused siblings wondered if they would ever see their older brothers again. A pall hung over the nation like a stalled low pressure system on a meteorologist's weather map.

As Philip Van Doren Stern approached the holiday season, he too was discouraged. He had written a short story that he felt confident would inspire a discouraged nation. But to his chagrin, he could not interest any magazine editors in his inspirational novella.

Stern called his story *The Greatest Gift*. It concerned a despondent man at Christmastime feeling as though his life had been a failure. While contemplating suicide on a bridge, he encounters a stranger who enables the man to experience a world in which he has never existed. The gift of a granted wish allows the discouraged individual to realize what a blessed life he has after all.

Stern, a writer, editor, and Civil War historian, decided to self-publish his 4,100 word short story. He printed 200 copies of the 24-page booklet and sent it out as his Christmas card to family and friends.

One of those who happened upon this unique Christmas greeting was Charles Koerner, the head of RKO Radio Pictures. Koerner bought the movie rights to the story for $50,000. After being adapted into a screenplay, *The Greatest Gift* was retitled, *It's a Wonderful Life* and released as a motion picture in December, 1946.

Curiously, Christmas provided the backdrop for the plot of Philip Stern's story. Christmas also provided the occasion for him to distribute his story as a Christmas card. The movie was released at Christmastime, and each Christmastime, *It's a Wonderful Life* is shown multiple times. Without Christmas we would never know the story of George Bailey. But more significantly, without Christmas our world would be drastically different.

The shock George Bailey felt as he wandered into the dark and depraved city limits of Pottersville is nothing when compared with what we would feel if our sin-infested planet had been denied the "Light of the World." What worked as a brilliant literary motif in Stern's story works as a startling exercise for those tempted to approach their faith casually. We would do well to ponder what our world would be like had Jesus Christ never been born.

British writer C. S. Lewis imagined such a dark, Christ-less planet in his brilliant children's story *The Lion, the Witch and the Wardrobe*. The world he conceived he called Narnia. Paralyzed under the frozen spell of the White Witch, it is a world in which it is "always winter but never Christmas."

Imagine such a world. Those who live in the northern and Midwest states know that winter is characterized by a bleak and cold season that tests a person's endurance and patience. The joys and traditions associated with Christmas give them something on which to focus while getting through the woes of winter.

A world devoid of such a focus would be a drab, dark world of beige lawns and brown fields in which bitter chilling winds blow through leafless tree branches. Freezing rain and blowing snow wreak havoc on the highways. Shoveled snow piled at the end of driveways turns grayish brown.

A world in which it is always winter but never Christmas would be a world in which the mail carrier stuffs your box with bills, bank statements, and third-class junk. No Christmas would mean no Christmas cards . . . and no caroling, Christmas concerts, parties, or gift giving, and other holiday traditions. The world would be devoid of twinkling lights and festive decorations. By definition, a world without Christmas would be a world without Jesus.

Have you ever tried to imagine what would be different in your *life* if Jesus had never been born? In addition to not having Christmas, we would have no Valentine's Day, St. Patrick's Day, Mardi Gras, Easter, Halloween, or Thanksgiving. Each one of those popular American holidays is based on (or somehow tied to) Christianity.

The absence of Jesus' presence in history would impact more than just our national holidays. It would create a world we would not recognize or value. For example, if Jesus had never been born, ancient Middle Eastern practices of infanticide and child sacrifice would likely have continued to be observed. Children would have been deemed as having little value. (Jesus elevated little ones to a previously unheard of position. Remember when even the disciples tried to divert the kids from crowding around him?)

If Jesus had never been born, women would have continued to be viewed primarily as property. (Before Jesus came on the religious scene, Jews offered daily prayer in which they thanked God they had not been born a Gentile, a woman, or a dog.)

If Jesus had never been born, God would be viewed as unapproachable, unknowable, and unobligated to forgive willful and unintentional transgressions. (If Jesus had never joined us on our human journey, if he had not lived a morally unblemished life and died an undeserved death and returned to life unexpectedly, we would not have the assurance of forgiveness and confidence of the Creator's acceptance.)

Had Jesus never been born, Simeon would have died a bitter old man. He had been promised he would see the Messiah before he left this earth.

Had Jesus never been born, the woman caught in adultery would have been stoned to death. The young daughter of the synagogue leader in Capernaum would have died. The corpse of the little boy in Nain would not have been resurrected, neither would Lazarus's lifeless body. Zacchaeus and Matthew would have died very wealthy and very unhappy tax collectors.

Had Jesus never been born, the cross would have been one of the most hated symbols anywhere. Without an empty grave providing the rest of the story, it would simply stand as the most inhumane form of capital punishment ever devised. No stained glass windows or gilded jewelry would ever be fashioned in the form of a cross.

Western civilization as we know it would be a far cry from what it is today. The teachings of the Sermon on the Mount and the Golden Rule would be missing in courts of law. Health care and education would be less important. The rights of the elderly would be overlooked or undermined. Jesus' presence and teachings informed all those things. His influence in the lives of those who came to call him Lord is mind boggling.

Can you imagine a world without the letters of Paul that contend for faith, hope, and (especially) love?

Can you imagine a world without the writings of Augustine and his example of being freed from the prison of a promiscuous lifestyle through the transforming power of the gospel?

Can you imagine a world without Telemachus, the fourth century Christian monk, who is credited with ending the gladiator games as a popular form of entertainment in Rome's Coliseum even though his protest of this practice cost him his life?

Can you imagine a world without St. Francis who celebrated members of the animal kingdom as gifts from the Creator worthy of care?

Can you imagine a world without the artistic masterpieces of the Renaissance largely influenced by the Christian message?

Can you imagine a world without a boat named the Mayflower transporting victims of religious persecution to the New World determined to populate a land where faith could be freely practiced?

Can you imagine a world without William Wilberforce and his Christian witness against slavery in Britain's Parliament?

Can you imagine a world without George Frideric Handel's immortal oratorio *Messiah*?

Can you imagine a world without Johann Sebastian Bach's inspiring music or his signature sentiment "Soli Deo Gloria" (to God alone be glory)?

Can you imagine science textbooks that do not include the findings of Copernicus, Kepler, Galileo, Descartes, Pascal, Newton, Faraday, and Mendel all of whom embraced the Christ of history and were shaped by his teachings?

Can you imagine a world without universities like Oxford, Cambridge, Harvard, Yale, Princeton, and many others that were founded by Christians to train Christians?

Can you imagine a world without Clara Barton and the lifesaving efforts that came from her Red Cross?

Can you imagine a world without General William Booth and his army of soldiers fighting on the frontlines of homelessness, hunger, and poverty?

Can you imagine a world without Bill Wilson's Twelve Steps or his Big Blue Book or the countless lives who have regained sobriety through the organization called Alcoholics Anonymous?

Can you imagine a world without Pastor Dietrich Bonhoeffer who led an underground movement against Hitler and was executed three weeks before the Allied Forces liberated the camp where he was imprisoned?

Can you imagine a world without Billy Graham crusading the world with a simple message of how Jesus can change a life?

Can you imagine a world without Martin Luther King, Jr. and his Christian message of liberty and justice for all?

Can you imagine a world without Mother Teresa and her Christ-like compassion to the dying on the dirty streets of Calcutta?

Can you imagine a world without Charles "Chuck" Colson and his gritty testimony of being born again from a Watergate criminal to a prison reformer?

Can you imagine a world without Bono, his music and his

commitment to justice, both of which have been shaped by his dependence on Jesus?

Trying to imagine a world in which Jesus was never born truly is like imagining winter with no Christmas. But there's no need to dwell on it. History points to the fact that Jesus *was* born. Biographies of his life have survived two millennia. Millions of his followers attest to the tangible change they have experienced because of a relationship with him. We can't explain the mysteries and wonders of our world without accepting the fact that Christ was born. Simply put, we can't imagine our world without the existence of Christmas.

QUESTIONS FOR REFLECTION:

1. What passages in the Old Testament hint of the birth of Jesus?

2. How would you live if Jesus had never been born?

3. Other than the examples mentioned in this chapter, what other influential Christian or event in history would drop out if Jesus had not been born?

4. Based on the impact Christians have had in politics, science, and art, how can the church continue to positively affect society?

Chapter 19

FINDING JESUS IN *IT'S A WONDERFUL LIFE*

Thus far, we've seen that looking for God in *It's a Wonderful Life* is a worthy pursuit. This much-loved movie has many spiritual images and faith applications. But do you know that Jesus himself makes an appearance in the film? It's true!

H.B. Warner, the actor who played Mr. Gower the pharmacist in *It's a Wonderful Life* also played the role of Jesus in the 1927 silent film, *King of Kings*. Cecil B. DeMille's highly-acclaimed motion picture featured the then fifty-two-year-old British-born actor. Great care was taken during the shooting of the movie, to separate "Jesus" from the public and his fellow actors. During the filming of the movie, Warner was driven to the set in a closed car with the blinds down and wore a black veil when he left the car for the set. He was even forced to eat his meals alone. While in costume, only DeMille was permitted to talk with him. The director even demanded that his "Jesus" refrain from activities deemed less than godly at the time. These included attending ball games, playing cards, frequenting night clubs, swimming, and riding in convertibles.

DeMille hoped that following the release of *King of Kings*, his lead actor would not appear in another movie playing other roles that would compromise his "holy" image. So Warner was required to sign an agreement that limited the parts he could play for a five-year period. Following *King of Kings*, Warner was primarily cast in dignified roles befitting his "divine" reputation. He had so distinguished himself in the role of Jesus that directors had difficulty thinking of him in an ordinary part.

Curiously, the plight of being typecast after playing Jesus on the big screen would also plague Jim Caviezel some eight decades later. Following his portrayal of the Son of God in *The Passion of the Christ*, Caviezel was overlooked for cinematic roles. A seven-year dry spell ended in the fall of 2011 when the born-again actor was cast in "Person of Interest," a serial drama on CBS television.

Director Frank Capra, however, was not willing to let DeMille's Christ be relegated to the realm of the divine. He wanted to bring the Son of God down to the level of struggling humanity. Thus the 71-year-old Warner was the perfect choice for playing the less than perfect nature of humankind.

So in the film we see Warner as a grief-stricken boss who becomes abusive to a young George Bailey after drinking too much. We also see him as an upstanding businessman who buys a grown-up George Bailey an extra-large suitcase for his much-anticipated vacation prior to starting college. We also see him as an indigent alcoholic who spent time in prison when he accidentally poisoned a child (this during the segment in the movie when George sees what the world would have been like without him. He wouldn't have been there to intercept Mr. Gower's near-fatal mistake).

This was an incarnation of sorts. No longer off-limits because of his identity as the Son of God, Warner was given the opportunity to mingle with the masses once again.

Here we have a picture of the divine Lord of glory coming down to our level and experiencing the flawed reality of a broken world in rebellion from its Creator. The Word (who created the planet we populate) became flesh and lived among us. Not aloof and hiding behind divine privileges, the One who would win our salvation tasted the bitter plight of our alienation himself.

In theological circles, this is known as the doctrine of *kenosis*, a Greek word that means emptying. It refers to the self-emptying of divinity to experience the plight of humanity. The Apostle Paul writes,

Who, being in very nature God, did not consider equality with God something to be used to his own advantage; rather, he made himself nothing by taking the very nature of a servant, being made in human likeness. And being found in appearance as a man, he humbled himself by becoming obedient to death—even death on a cross! (Philippians 2:6-8)

In the movie itself, George Bailey's character illustrates such "self-effacing" humility. There is an unforgettable scene in the Bailey Building and Loan including a meeting after the death of George's father, Peter Bailey. Mr. Potter, a member of the board with self-serving motives, belittles the business practices and moves that the business be abolished. George is furious and expresses an emotional appeal to save the company while defending his father's honor—leaving the board room in a huff. He has delayed his college education already by four years and now is a week late for school. Ernie the taxi driver is waiting to take him to the train station.

But a commotion in the boardroom ends with someone intercepting George before he catches his cab. The board will vote to keep the Building and Loan going as long as George agrees to stay and run the business. He agrees. He alone can save it. Having earned the right to follow his own dreams, George is hooked on the horns of a dilemma. He resists the temptation to put his agenda first. Denying himself, George takes up the servant's basin and towel and serves those who need him the most.

There again we find Jesus in the movie. After all, the Savior said, ". . . the Son of Man did not come to be served, but to serve, and to give his life as a ransom for many" (Matthew 20:28). And again, "Whoever wants to be my disciple must deny themselves and take up their cross daily and follow me" (Luke 9:23).

QUESTIONS FOR REFLECTION:

1. How do you feel about the measures Cecil B. DeMille took to keep H.B. Warner from interacting with the rest of the cast?

2. What correlation do you see between that and the biblical injunction to "come out from them and be separate" (2 Corinthians 6:17)?

3. The pressure of playing Jesus was too much for H.B. Warner. The stress drove him to abusing alcohol. What kind of stress do you experience when you try to live like Jesus in your own strength apart from the Holy Spirit?

4. Imagine the surprise when the actor who played Christ in *King of Kings* showed up as Mr. Gower in *It's a Wonderful Life*. What are some unexpected ways you might surprise people (who know you are a Christ-follower) by showing up in their lives?

Chapter 20

LITTLE GOLD STATUES DON'T TELL THE WHOLE STORY

*I*t's a *Wonderful Life* was nominated for five Academy Awards in 1947: Best Picture, Best Director, Best Actor, Best Editing, and Best Sound Recording. By the time Oscar's long night of celebrating was over, the Capra film had been shut out. It didn't win one little gold statue. The Best Picture honors went to *The Best Years of Our Lives* directed by William Wyler, Capra's partner at Liberty Films.

The outcome was a real disappointment to Frank Capra. The winner of multiple Oscars believed *IAWL* to have been his best effort to date. But some critics thought the film too Pollyanna against the backdrop of the realities exposed in the war.

Although moviegoers were mostly positive about the film, it was not a smash hit and lost just shy of $500,000. The movie debuted in only a few theatres the week before Christmas, 1946. It was not released nationally until July of 1947. By that time, Frank Capra's Liberty Films had been sold to Paramount Pictures. When all the statistics had been tallied, *It's a Wonderful Life* did not have such a wonderful life. Variety's list of movies released in 1946-47 found the Capra castaway in twenty-seventh place.

But as both *The Wizard of Oz* and *Citizen Kane* proved, movies thought to be disappointing flops when first released can be prematurely (and wrongly) judged. Such was the case of Frank Capra's gem. But then something unexpected happened.

In 1974, almost thirty years after its release, the film's copyright protection expired due to a clerical error. As a result, the movie fell into public domain, and television stations were able to show it without any royalty fee. During the 70s, stations across the nation aired the movie at Christmastime over and over again. Amazingly, millions and millions of fans fell in love with the film. By 1994, when NBC TV purchased exclusive rights, *It's a Wonderful Life* had become a timeless Christmas classic.

Today some seven decades after its debut, *It's a Wonderful Life* is on the American Film Institute's list of "100 Greatest Movies Ever Made" (coming in at #11) and was awarded the #1 spot on the list of "Most Inspiring Movies of All Time."

Just desserts can be delayed in more than just the movies. This kind of deferred recognition is also referenced in the New Testament. Hebrews 11, often called the biblical hall of fame, features a list of names from Bible history. Beginning with Abel, Enoch, Noah, Abraham, and Sarah, we are invited to consider the way each individual trusted God instead of allowing the circumstances they faced to define their view of reality. The writer continues to walk through the pages of Israel's ancient history. His guided tour reminds us of Isaac and Jacob's faith as well as that of Joseph, Moses, and Rahab.

Gideon, Barak, Samson, Jephthah, David, Samuel, and all the prophets are spotlighted in addition to those who are not named but whose godly trust is praised:

> . . . who through faith conquered kingdoms, administered justice, and gained what was promised; who shut the mouths of lions, quenched the fury of the flames, and escaped the edge of the sword; whose weakness was turned to strength; and who became powerful in battle and routed foreign armies. Women received back their dead, raised to life again. There were others who were tortured, refusing to be released so that they might gain an even better resurrection. Some faced jeers and flogging, and even chains and imprisonment. They were put to death by stoning; they were sawed

> *in two; they were killed by the sword. They went about in sheepskins and*
> *goatskins, destitute, persecuted and mistreated. (vv. 33-37)*

These people, who provided human faces to an abstract theological doctrine called faith, faced challenges head on. Their lives were full as well as fulfilling. You might say they each lived a wonderful life. But just like the movie, they were not given their just desserts. In many cases, they were overlooked in addition to being underappreciated. Our tour guide in this "Hall of Fame" is like one of the few critics that gave *It's a Wonderful Life* two thumbs up. As far as the writer is concerned, the grueling hardships faith demanded of these heroes put them in a league of their own. We read . . .

> *The world was not worthy of them. They wandered in deserts and mountains,*
> *living in caves and in holes in the ground. (Hebrews 11:38)*

Then the writer adds a postscript. Although the faith-performance on history's stage of these outstanding individuals was Oscar-worthy, they were denied their reward in life. They didn't receive that to which they were entitled. So even in death they were called on to exercise faith in what God had promised. Some might describe it as "deferred gratification." The Hall of Fame chronicler puts it this way:

> *These were all commended for their faith, yet none of them received what had*
> *been promised, since God had planned something better for us so that only*
> *together with us would they be made perfect. (vv. 39-40)*

In other words, time will reveal God's pleasure. Furthermore, God intends that their awards ceremony be delayed until those who follow their example receive their own expressions of worth.

To that end, the writer of Hebrews carries on without interruption as he begins chapter 12 (remember, the original manuscript had no chapter breaks):

> *Therefore, since we are surrounded by such a great cloud of witnesses, let us*
> *throw off everything that hinders and the sin that so easily entangles. And*
> *let us run with perseverance the race marked out for us. (v. 1)*

In other words, since we are aware of these who have honored God with their lives so courageously yet selflessly, let us follow their lead.

The writer suggests that this cast of award-winning actors and actresses (who have provided us critically-acclaimed performances) are now sitting in the audience cheering us on as we bring faith to life. This crowd of spectators who watch us far outnumbers those in the Kodak theatre who gather each year for the Academy Awards ceremony.

But, since these heroes of the faith have not received their rewards, their reputations are dwarfed by those prematurely praised as the giants of society. To most of the world, the accomplishments of God's faithful servants were not all that special. In fact, those who look at Israel's faithful see miserable failures.

That's why it is essential to remember that time is the revealer of lasting worth. Statues and trophies, no matter how large or many, do not alone determine success or influence—in Hollywood or Holy Scripture; in life or in death.

Mountain Grove Cemetery in Bridgeport, Connecticut, is the final resting place of Phineas T. Barnum, the famous circus promoter of the nineteenth century. The circus king's tombstone is an imposing monolith rising an impressive 20 feet in the air. Such a marker celebrates the successes and popularity of the one who is credited with creating "the greatest show on earth."

Just a stone's throw from Barnum's tombstone is the place where the hymn-writer Fanny Jane Crosby is interred. In stark contrast to the circus king's mountain of granite, Crosby's simple grave has these words engraved on a small marble marker: "Aunt Fanny—She Hath Done What She Could."

Suffice it to say that what she could was more than amazing. Blinded as an infant as a result of negligence on the part of a doctor, this remarkable woman went on to write more than 5,000 hymns including "To God Be The Glory," "Rescue the Perishing," "Safe in the Arms of Jesus," and "Blessed Assurance." She lived to be one month shy of 95 years of age. But relatively few Americans knew of her prolific pen compared to the heralded heroics of Mr. Barnum.

During the years both individuals lived, P.T. Barnum was unquestionably more popular and influential than F.J. Crosby. His press clippings and honors far exceeded the little known gospel poet. Much like *It's a Wonderful Life*, Crosby's enduring (and endearing) contribution to culture would only be realized and celebrated years later.

A century after Fanny's death, her legacy has far outdistanced the circus king. Though sightless, she was *not* blind to the matchless value of faith. With pen in hand, she raised our level of understanding of a God we cannot see while giving us a vocabulary of praise. Refusing to be bitter for her plight of endless night, Miss Fanny Jane accepted her cross as a privilege of sharing in the sufferings of Christ.

For her, faith continued to be the assurance of things hoped for and the evidence of things unseen (Hebrews 11:1). Fanny Crosby died not fully realizing the impact her rhyming words would have on individuals long after she was buried in her simple grave. Like those mentioned in the concluding verses of Hebrews 11, she too would not experience the reward she was due. But the hymns she penned bore witness to the blessed assurance known by the heroes of the faith who died with the confidence that God was aware of their contribution to the Kingdom.

No, you really can't measure a movie's popularity by the number of little gold statues it is awarded the year it is released. Nor can a person's greatness be adequately measured by the size of her gravestone. What matters most is what is concluded when time has had its say.

QUESTIONS FOR REFLECTION:

1. What do you make from the fact that *The Wizard of Oz*, *Citizen Kane*, and *It's a Wonderful Life* all were considered failures when they first debuted?

2. In Romans 8:18-19 the apostle Paul refers to present-day suffering eventually becoming something wonderful. In Galatians 6:9, he refers to those who don't give up will reap a well-deserved harvest. What other Bible verses can you identify that support the concept of waiting for the final say?

3. Who are some modern-day counterparts to P.T. Barnum and F. J. Crosby? What are the trappings of success and failure respectively?

4. What do you make of the phrase the writer of Hebrews uses to describe the trailblazers of faith: "The world was not worthy of them"? What does that say about the society and believers' lives?

Epilogue

In the very last scene of the movie, George is overwhelmed by the outpouring of love and generosity demonstrated by those who have learned of his missing funds. While standing near the Christmas tree twinkling with lights, he sees a copy of *The Adventures of Tom Sawyer* in the basket filled with donations contributed by family, friends, neighbors, and customers. Reaching in, he opens the book and reads this inscription inside the front cover: *"No man is a failure who has friends."* It is signed by Clarence, his angelic visitor.

Those eight words really spell out the message of the movie. From start to finish we are eyewitnesses to a man who invests in friendship without regard for return. And then when it appears that his account has been depleted, he discovers a simple truth: When you make deposits in the lives of others, you aren't always aware of the compounding interest that is taking place. But the bottom line reveals a wealth that exceeds your expectations.

Throughout Scripture we find friendship celebrated. Jesus refused to go it alone. He surrounded himself with twelve friends and sent them out two by two on ministry expeditions. Abraham invested in friendship with his nephew Lot. Moses needed Aaron. Daniel treasured time with Shadrach, Meshach, and Abednego. David valued his companion, Jonathan. Elijah journeyed with Elisha. Paul teamed with Barnabas and John Mark, as well as Silas and Luke. No wonder the apostle Paul dipped his pen in his ink pot one last time before scratching his final thoughts to his friends in Galatia. He knew that having friends keeps us from failing at what matters most in life: "Carry each other's burdens...."

Long before the apostles attested to the value of friendship, King Solomon appraised it as his stock in trade:

> Two are better than one, because they have a good return for their labor: If either of them falls down, one can help the other up. But pity anyone who falls and has no one to help them up. Also, if two lie down together, they will keep warm. But how can one keep warm alone? Though one may be overpowered, two can defend themselves. A cord of three strands is not quickly broken. (Ecclesiastes 4:9-12)

SO BLESSED ARE WE

So long ago God whispered in a garden,
it is not good for us to be alone.
We need companionship and affirmation.
Life can be hard, our hearts as hard as stone.
We long to be both understood and valued,
encouraged in the gifts by which we're known.

So steep, so difficult the trail we're climbing.
At times we wonder if we can go on.
We slip and fall. At times we're even bleeding.
Our journey can seem tortuous and long.
But when we walk in step with one another,
the darkest night becomes a hopeful dawn.

So let us be transparent with each other,
confessing things we hope for, fear and need.
Without the insight that a friend can offer,
we're often blind to ego, lust and greed.
Temptation's hold on us is strangely weakened
when, linked in prayer, we boldly intercede.

So blessed are we to be joined to each other
on this adventure that we share as one.
The curse of loneliness has now been broken.
The joy of Heaven seems to have begun.
What God intended for His chosen offspring
we know firsthand through friendship with His Son.

—Greg Asimakoupoulos